Cover art and design by Katie Borkin

2

3

Optimal Freedom

4

Optimal Freedom

by Jeff Rout

How to Maximize Individual Freedom and Individual Control
over the Government

Domino Effect Publishing

6

First Printing September 2017

ISBN 978-0-9867593-5-2

Thank you Dad for all the help on this book.

8

Table of Contents

Preface..11

People Should Be Free from Unreasonable Restrictions on How to Live Their Own Lives...13

The Tripod of Liberty..18

Individual Freedoms...21

The Freedom to Think and Believe, and to Express Those Thoughts and Beliefs...30

Representative Democracy or Elected Oligarchy?.................36

Use a Deferred Direct Democracy to Maximize Individual Power over Government...43

Citizen Initiative..49

Citizen Veto Power via Referendum: Ultimate Power over Government is Equally in the Hands of the Individual Citizens 57

Recall Legislation...66

Laws Should Be Created, Controlled, and Enforced as Locally as Is Practical..77

Localism Doesn't Mean Left Wing or Right Wing Politics....81

Localism Means More People Get the Government They Want 84

Governments Can Attempt Innovative Solutions with Localism 91

Local Governments Can Implement Locally Effective Solutions..94

Nations Do Not Need a Coast to Be Sustainable....................96

Nations Do Not Need All Their Own Resources to Succeed 100

Small Nations Can Manage Their Own Currency if Need Be
....102

Immigration Should Be Controlled Locally..........................107

Localism Is Not Infinitely Reducible....................................110

The Minimum and Maximum Size for a Good Locally
Controlled Government...113

Localism Can Still Mean Cooperation with Others..............116

Small Governments Can Still Protect Citizens with an
Effective Military...120

Optimal Freedom Resists Totalitarianism.............................126

We Can Still Be the Same Country, Even If We Are Each Our
Own Sovereign Nations..128

Large Countries Should Consider Transferring Sovereign
Powers to Local Levels...136

Support for Local Control of Government Is Growing.........139

The Primary Role of Government Is to Protect Its Citizens. 143

Limiting Government Ability to Coerce the Public..............150

Conclusion...156

Preface

The purpose of this book is to attempt to prove the proposition that every person should live under a system of government that maximizes human prosperity and advancement; and that the best method to achieve those is with an optimal design of individual freedom.

I make some statements that could be considered aggressively assertive. I consider my statements in this book defensible. This book builds on some assumptions that I don't attempt to prove. I assume that reducing human suffering is good. I assume that oppression and coercion are bad. I take a position that we would be free if we don't have other people dominating us. I don't prove these assumptions as I think that most people would agree with them without proof. Also, I want this book to be short enough to be readable without excessive effort. This is already rather dry material and to add a proof for each step would increase this book's size about 3 times over.

Also for the sake of brevity, this is not meant to be comprehensive. It is meant to form a foundation of an idea that we can build on to further advance human flourishing, freedom and democratic power.

We often take our freedom for granted, but it is not guaranteed to us. Freedom as we now have it has only existed for a very short period, and there are many forces working to take it away from us. This book gives some of my thoughts on how we can reduce the risk of losing the freedom we have, and expand it even further.

People Should Be Free from Unreasonable Restrictions on How to Live Their Own Lives

Imagine a person living completely alone without any other human contact and without any government. That person would be as free as a bird. There would be no one taking anything from that person or limiting what that person could do. In a sense, that person could be considered to be the government as there isn't another one. That person has 100% control over the laws and policies of the government. That person is free.

Freedom doesn't mean being able to do whatever you want. That person isn't free to do whatever they want to do. The freedom to do whatever you want to do doesn't honestly exist. We are limited by the resources and circumstances around us. We are limited in our choices by ethical restrictions to not hurt other people, and to not violate their rights and freedoms.

We aren't free to buy what we can't afford. We aren't free from having horrible events happen to us. We are free to make our own choices, but even those choices are limited to our circumstances. Our family, our job, our health, our culture, and our relationships can all restrain our choices. That is just an inevitable part of life. But we must avoid having superfluous government interference that also inhibits our choices artificially.

Freedom means being free from laws that restrict your thoughts, speech, or actions, except where your actions would harm or cause significant risk of harm to others, or restrict the rights and freedoms of others. That is the same level of freedom that a person living in solitude enjoys. We should be as close as possible to that freedom as we can reasonably get.

We can't all live in solitude such as that, however. We need to have laws on how we can interact with each other. That means limitations by society on what we are allowed to do. What should we choose the basis of those laws to be?

We should want each person to have as little force and coercion placed on their lives as the person who lives freely in solitude. This accepts that there need be some force. We must forcibly enforce homicide laws, for example. But we want to keep those restrictions to a reasonable minimum. That minimum is live and let live. So long as your actions are not causing harm or significant risk to others, or take away the freedom of others, do what you want to do.

When there is any group of people, they must make some agreement on how they will interact, even if that agreement is unspoken and informal. We only have two possible relationships: one of tyranny, force, and oppression; or one of negotiation, persuasion, and compromise.

There is a tendency in humanity to move towards tyranny. This isn't because most people want to dominate others who disagree with them. Most people follow a mantra closer to live and let live. But there are always a few people very willing to abandon a live and let live philosophy in favour of oppressing others to live as commanded instead. They create the laws they want because they are the strongest and are both willing and able to hurt those that oppose them. In all reality, this has been the historic norm.

If the majority of people follow a peaceful 'live and let live' belief, then how can humanity tend towards tyranny? It does this because it only takes a few people who are both willing and able to enforce their dictatorship to create that dictatorship. If the peaceful people don't have the will, power or courage to defend their peaceful lifestyle, then it will be destroyed and replaced with that tyranny. As Edmund Burke said, 'The only thing necessary for the triumph of evil is for good men to do nothing.'

Tyrannies don't work for the optimal solution to all people. They use their power to force their political will on others. So we find more people are unhappy with the government and life in general under a tyranny. Rather than working to maximize human prosperity, they bring about increased human suffering.

Life under freedom is the opposite. Life under freedom means that a person is able to try to maximize their prosperity without unreasonable restriction from the government. So long as they are not harming others, do as you wish.

Tyrants typically don't want to be tyrannized themselves. They are very dreadful hypocrites in their beliefs. They want to say whatever they want but want to restrict others in their speech. They want the power to have exactly the policies in government they want but don't want others to have the same level of power for themselves. There's no universal application in tyranny. It's entirely one-sided. There's no do unto others as you want them to do to you – a good basis for determining what is a universally moral position. Indeed, morality has nothing to do with tyranny. Tyranny is all about force, coercion, and violence.

Peaceful people see this differently. They don't want to be hurt or oppressed themselves, and therefore they apply a philosophy of not hurting and not oppressing others. They don't want to be coerced, so they will not apply coercion to others.

Like a schoolyard bully who tells others what to say or he will beat them up, a tyrannical government controls the speech of citizens. It doesn't allow them the freedom to share ideas and try to improve the general knowledge and understanding of society. It forces them to say the one approved speech.

But under optimal freedom, there is no bully in the government. It protects the right for each person to speak their mind. People can say something that might go against conventional thought, shock others, or criticize the government. They are still protected by the law.

Some people say live and let live. It's a good saying. It says let's not force our beliefs on others. Let us have our beliefs and let others have theirs. This type of philosophy is very peaceful. It doesn't threaten violence and if universally followed no violence could really exist. Live and let live ultimately means peace. Tyranny is the opposite. Tyranny means live and oppress others. It is never content with letting others live their own lives as they want to. Tyranny forces a life style on others, and if they dissent, they are attacked. Since people are all different, and always will be different, and since tyranny doesn't peacefully accept those differences, tyranny never means peace. Tyranny means violent oppression.

We need a philosophy of governing that focuses on this creed and holds it sacred: Every person should have the minimal amount of force or coercion placed on them by the government as to how they will live their own lives as is reasonably possible.

With a creed such as this, no one will be prevented by the government from doing what makes them most content; unless that action would cause injury or significant risk to others, or take away the freedom of others. Without a creed like this, there is no means to avoid having one group of people being able to manipulate the law to exert their will on others. It isn't good to be oppressed by others, and it isn't moral to be the oppressor.

While humanity tends towards tyranny, this tendency doesn't help humanity. Tyrannies never work for the benefit of all or even the most people, they only work for the benefit of the tyrants themselves. They work with oppression and violence. Every person should be as free from coercion from others as is reasonably possible. So long as a person's actions are not hurting others, let them think, say, and do as they wish.

The Tripod of Liberty

The nature of freedom is reducible to one basic concept. Every person on Earth should have a minimum amount of force placed on them by others as to how they will live their own lives. To achieve this, we need to have these three elements of liberty: every person must have their individual rights and freedoms protected; security against violence; and every voter must have an equal and maximal control over the laws, policies, and taxes of the government.

Each of these elements is essential for people to have as much control over their own lives as possible. Where any of these elements are weak, our freedom is also weak. If we have any of these removed we lose freedom completely.

Without individual rights and freedoms, one immediately has very little control over their own life. They are not free to think or believe what they choose to nor to say it. If they are limited in their very thoughts and speech, then they are also fundamentally limited in how they can take any action that they choose for themselves as well.

Individual rights are essential to the concept of liberty as without them a society can simply force a person how to live on the basis of majority rule.

Being free from government coercion over the individual is a fundamental element of freedom, but it isn't the only element. Indeed, without the others, it has very little power or influence on freedom.

Without also having maximum control over the laws that govern their lives, people remain at the whim and control of others and are not their own masters. In order to have the least government coercion on their lives, each person must also have the absolute maximum amount of power over the laws that govern them as is reasonably possible. With maximum control over the laws that govern their lives, they have the maximum ability to have those laws not interfere with their lives and to reflect their opinions and objectives in government. Democracy doesn't function only as a means to protect and preserve freedom. Democracy is an essential element of freedom. If you cannot control the laws that govern your life you also cannot control your choices in life.

No voter should have more of a say in the laws than any others. Tyrants would have the maximum control over the law that is possible. But that would only be for them, not for all. So one reasonable limitation to the idea of maximum control over the law is that it should be the maximum that can be equally shared and enjoyed by all the voters.

The last leg of the tripod is security from violence. Both of the above freedoms can be destroyed if there isn't adequate security that protects citizens from violence. People cannot be free if they are under constant fear of violent attack.

Individual freedoms can't be exercised if others are using threats to take it away from them. Democratic power can become meaningless if there is violence being used to coerce people and manipulate the democratic process. And we are not free if we are able to be invaded and conquered by a foreign nation because we lacked the proper military strength to dissuade such invasion. Freedom isn't based on just one or two aspects of individual freedom or control of the government. We need every leg of the tripod in order to have real liberty. If any of them are weak, each of the others also becomes weaker. If any are taken away, the entire structure collapses.

Individual Freedoms

Democracy generally means that the majority rules. It's a good policy which brings about the maximum amount of agreement on the basis of the law. But it isn't enough on its own.

The rights of the minority must be protected. While it must be the majority that determines the law, that majority must never have the ability to trample on the rights and freedoms of the minority. The majority must also not have the power to put a separate set of laws or application of the law that treats the minority differently from others, or vice versa.

Rule of the majority can quickly become a tyranny of the majority. Rule of the majority can mean that the majority vote that the minority can't have any rights. Rule of the majority can mean the people can vote for another person to be forced out of society. Rule of majority can mean that people can vote for another person to be killed. Today we might think of that as a hyperbole, but we should remember being voted to leave society is what ostracism originally meant. And we should remember that Socrates was killed on a vote of his peers.

Therefore, law must be tempered with fundamental rights and freedoms.

No society is just if its people are not free. If the government can take away our home from us because we might say something that is unpopular, as Socrates did, then we are certainly not living under optimal freedom. A democracy which doesn't respect and actively protect individual rights and freedoms has no more legitimacy than a dictatorship. To deny people their freedom over their own lives is deeply immoral and unjust. While we may have thought this to be an obvious truth, more than half the world does not live in freedom today. Additionally, there are coordinated forces acting in today's free nations to systematically erode those freedoms.

This concept transcends a tyranny of the majority, and includes a tyranny of a party, or of a single person. Just as the majority must not have any power to trample the rights and freedoms of others, neither must any party. Where any party can prevent others from the free exercise of their rights, that is the path to subjugation.

Rule of majority is therefore a good policy for determining the law, indeed it is probably the best policy, but it isn't sufficient on its own. We also need to have laws restricted so that they cannot infringe on individual freedoms and rights.

With unassailable rights and freedoms people are protected against oppression from the government. Despite their beliefs being in the minority, they are free to say what they believe. What rights and freedoms must the people have?

They must be free to consider or believe any thoughts.

The government must have no ability to condemn them for their thoughts in any way whatsoever. The government must not have any ability to condemn thoughts with laws, policies, taxes, motions, stigma, or any other means.

Indeed, there is no ethical basis for the government to be in the business of policing thoughts in any way. The government's role is not to tell citizens what to think, but to listen to what citizens say, and obey the instructions of the majority.

They must be free to say what they think or express themselves with only very few, reasonable, restrictions.

One reasonable restriction is speech that is intended to instruct others to imminent criminal activity and is likely to do so.

We also want to have the potential for civil court and criminal court action for speech which has caused a panic leading to damage over a false claim.

And lastly we want speech which has caused damage to another person's reputation with a false claim to be actionable with a civil court dispute or a criminal offense in rare circumstances.

In all cases, truth must be a defense.

Other than these few and reasonable exceptions, there must be no other limitations at all on free speech.

They must be free to negotiate terms of employment.

They should be free to negotiate compensation for their job. They should be free to choose to decline a job for less compensation than they want, or for any other reason. They must be free to choose to negotiate terms of employment collectively with other employees.

They must be free to choose their sexual preferences.

Whatever consenting adults chose to do sexually in private is none of the government's business. The government should have no power to enact policy or law to discriminate against any sexual practice between consenting adults.

They must be free to associate or to not associate with whomever they choose.

People must have the right to choose whom they associate with. They must also not be forced by the government to associate with those they would otherwise choose not to.

They must be free to assemble peacefully.

Like the freedom of association, there must be no unreasonable limitation on the public's ability to assemble where they are not limiting the free movement.

If we don't have the right of peaceful assembly, our right to association and to meet people that share our political objectives is limited to meeting in our own homes. There is no freedom of association without peaceful assembly, and there are no real democratic rights if people cannot share their political opinions.

They must be free to choose any religion they like.

Freedom of religion exists as a right that is already protected if people have freedom of thought, belief, speech, expression, association, and assembly, even if freedom of religion is not directly expressed that way. If people have these freedoms then everything reasonably required in freedom of religion already exists.

Their freedom of thought and belief protect their religious beliefs. Their freedom of speech and expression protect their right to share their religious beliefs and to wear religious clothing. The freedom of association and assembly protects their right to share their beliefs with each other and form congregations.

Since everything one needs to have a religion is already included in the above freedoms, freedom of religion is a redundancy. The only reason to have a separate freedom of religion is to reinforce the concept that one is not persecuted for religious beliefs. Given the prevalence of religious persecution in history, that redundancy is well warranted.

They must be free to have any opinion on any religion, and must be free to express that opinion without any type of coercion or punishment from the government. They must be free to like, or love, or dislike, or hate any religious belief – or have no opinion on them at all – or have any opinion in between these. Anything other than this is religious persecution and nothing less than a grievous and terrible violation of human rights.

Freedom of religion does not give a right to violate laws due to religious belief. The law must be universal and all must be equal before the law regardless of religion. Just as a person is not legally allowed to commit human sacrifice due to religious belief, a person must not be allowed to credibly instruct others to commit a crime and have religious freedom as a protection against that.

If there is ever a religious requirement that is not permitted in the law, such as human sacrifice, the use of peyote, the carrying of a knife, etc., then those laws should be examined. If the religious act is untenable, as human sacrifice would be, then there should not be any accommodation for that act based on religion. If the religious act can be reasonably included, then reasonable work arounds should be used that give as much leeway as possible for the ability to perform their religious beliefs while maintaining law and order with equality before the law. Perhaps allow everyone to carry an unsharpened blade not exceeding a certain length which would fulfill the Sikh requirement for a Kirpan. Perhaps allow peyote for anyone, but require a license which is not determined by religion for its use or distribution.

The government has a responsibility to ensure that its laws do not infringe unreasonably on the religious practices of others. Where it does, the laws should be examined and perhaps changed so that the religious practice can continue without needing an exception to the law based on religion. If the law can be reasonably changed so that this practice is universally allowed, regardless of religion, then change the law. If the law could not be universally allowed to all people, then keep it illegal regardless of religious beliefs. Do not create religious exemptions to the law. A law with a religious exemption is a system of law that will prosecute some but not others for the same act based only on their religion. That is religious persecution. The law must be universally applied and all must be equal before the law.

Freedom of religion doesn't mean that others must revere or admire your religious beliefs. You are free to revere or admire any religion you choose, but others must not be forced to think as you do on that religion.

They must be free to buy, own, or sell their property.

People should be free to choose to buy what they want; with a few minimal exceptions based on immediate danger to others.

They should be free to own their possessions and not be subject to confiscation without fair and due process. They should be free to choose to sell their property or to not sell their property. When buying or selling, they should be free to accept a price, attempt to negotiate a different price, or to reject a price.

Rights and freedoms must never by used as a means to force others to any action except to not interfere with you.

Every right has a corresponding duty. With freedom of speech comes a duty to not prevent others from speaking. With freedom of thought there comes a duty to not coerce thoughts and opinions on others. With freedom of religion there comes a duty to not persecute others based on religion.

The common thread of each right, freedom, and duty is that it involves not preventing others from exercising their rights. It doesn't involve a duty to assist them. Freedom of speech means that people have the right to write whatever they wish with only the few limitations listed above. That right doesn't install a duty on others to help you write. There is no obligation on others to provide you with the means to speak. Their duty is limited to not stopping you.

While we must have freedom of speech, we must not have the power to force others to listen to us. There is no right for others to listen to you.

We must not have the power to restrict the freedom of speech of others because we find it disagreeable. There is no right to not be offended.

While we must have freedom of religion, we must not have the power to force others to revere or admire a religion. We must not have the power to force others to obey the tenants of our religion. There is no right to religious conformity.

We may agree that we want universal health care. That doesn't mean we have a right to make another person provide us with health care. We may agree that we want universal education. That doesn't mean we have a right to make another person provide education. Rights and freedoms are restrictions on what the government and other people can force on you; they are not

The concept of individual freedoms is not universally accepted.

Indeed, it has only the level, strength, and prevalence of belief since the Renaissance. It was this Enlightenment that started the path that the individual must be free from control, and it was this that brought about the greatest flourishing of human freedom and prosperity that the world has ever seen.

Even today, freedom is not enjoyed by the majority of people. Most people live in societies that are not free. And in societies that are free, there are those that wish to take it away and impose their belief structure instead.

A democracy that respects individual rights and freedoms means that law is created by persuasion, negotiation, and compromise rather than by force. Democracy means ballots, not bullets. There is no way to force law against the majority in a democracy, it is determined by the people. The only way to affect the law would be to persuade the people rather than to force them.

But there are people within every society that would prefer to use force and violence to impose their desires, whether or not the majority disagrees. They reject individual freedoms because they want to force their opinion of government on everyone, and to silence any disagreement. They don't want a free society, they want a society that must obey them.

Of those who want to live in an unfree society, we don't usually hear them say 'I want to live in a society where I can't be what I want or do what I want." No, the purveyors of a dominating, commanding society want to be free themselves, they just want others to also be under their command as well. While they never word it this way, they essentially say, 'I want to live in a society that is what I want it to be, and everyone who disagrees must obey or be punished.' Ultimately, their real objective is to dominate other human beings and force their will upon others.

For every person to have maximum freedom over their own lives they must have the maximum amount of control over the laws that govern them, while also not restricting or limiting the ability for others to have the laws they want as well.

These freedoms are essential for individual prosperity as well as for equality before the law. They must be protected and cherished for they will be at risk. There will always be those who would take away the freedom of a person for the benefit of their own oppressive agenda.

The Freedom to Think and Believe, and to Express Those Thoughts and Beliefs

The freedom to have your own thoughts and beliefs, and to express them is fundamental to the success and prosperity of both the individual and society. Freedom of speech is so fundamental to all other freedoms and to democracy that we should have only the minimum of limitations on it.

Speech shouldn't be credibly intended to instruct others to imminent criminal activity and is likely to do so. This is a reasonable restriction as we do not want to have a society that is prone to violence.

We want to limit damage to people or property which is instigated by false statements that lead people into a panic. False statements that are clearly the cause of a panic should be actionable.

And lastly we want speech which has caused damage to another person's reputation with a false claim which caused them a loss to be actionable with a civil court dispute or a criminal offense in rare circumstances.

In all cases, truth must be a defense.

Other than these few and reasonable exceptions, there must be no other limitations at all on free speech.

Free speech helps us get closer to truth.

Freedom of thought and speech encourages concepts to mingle and compete against each other in the marketplace of ideas. We understand that we do now know everything. If we disallow ideas that are against the commonly accepted belief, if we only allow ideas that echo what we already believe, then we cannot advance beyond our current level of understanding.

All human intellectual progress has been from a thought that dissented against common belief. Socrates, Galileo, Newton, and Einstein each brought a new idea that ran against the commonly accepted beliefs of their times. If societies suppressed those ideas, as Copernicus' and Galileo's attempted to, then our society would not have benefited from the increase in knowledge each new idea brought. Diversity of thought is essential to the progress of our understanding.

We must allow all speech, even that which we would consider false.

Some might say we should only allow ideas that are true. This isn't a practical solution as we do not have perfect knowledge and cannot, therefore, perfectly know what is true. We cannot know which ideas are true and which are false until they are shared, explored, and challenged. Even after that, what we now consider true could in the future be considered false.

When a person says we should only allow speech that is true what that really means is we should only allow speech that is generally considered true and we should forbid speech that is contrary to general opinion. Every advancement in human knowledge began with an idea that was once considered false. Society stated that Copernicus and Galileo's ideas were not true. That we should not allow speech that is false is precisely the position taken by the tribunals that tried Galileo and Copernicus in order to protect the ideas they approved. Those ideas of the judges were ultimately proven false. Even the worst of tyrants will agree with freedom of speech when that speech agrees with them.

We will get many ideas that are false. That is unavoidable. But even the false ideas strengthen society. We are able to examine and deliberate the new concepts, and if they prove false, by eliminating them as a possibility we still grow stronger in our understanding.

We cannot move closer to the truth without new and differing opinions. We condemn ourselves and our societies to stagnant ignorance if we oppress the voices of those that disagree with us. The only means to truly advance human understanding is to accept, cherish, and defend the freedoms of thought and expression for those who disagree with us.

The government should have no power at any time to tell people what is true or false. It must have no power to restrict speech to what it accepts as true. Just as a seed needs water to grow, society needs freedoms of thought and speech to advance.

Freedom of speech protects minority populations.

Minority populations are not limited by the government on what they can say where there is free speech.

This allows them to openly discuss any issues that they might be facing. Without free speech, the government can simply forbid them from expressing this concerns and give them no method of improving their situation.

Coercion of opinion is both unethical and ineffective.

It was abhorrently immoral to torture people who didn't agree with the religious beliefs of the Spanish Inquisition, it is equally immoral to attack a person who has thoughts that differ from our own. There are no two people, alive or dead, that share all the same thoughts and opinions. Every person disagrees with every other person about something. I wouldn't want others to hurt or force me to silence me for not agreeing with them on any subject. So I must not hurt or silence others when they disagree with me. One's thoughts are the most basic and intimate manifestation of who one is. Controlling another person's thoughts or speech is among the most totalitarian actions there are.

Ironically, suppressing an opinion that differs from our own gives credence to the idea being suppressed. Nonsensical ideas are not usually disallowed. They are allowed but simply dismissed. But when an idea is suppressed people wonder why. They naturally think there might be something to this idea; if people that want you to not believe it won't allow you to even hear it.

Free speech can prevent violence, as it gives a peaceful method to achieve change.

Additionally, the idea being suppressed might be of a great importance to the people unable to speak it. It might be more important to them than life and death. When we suppress an idea like that, we remove the ability for people to advance such an important cause peacefully. The only method they then have is violence. Suppressing speech does not kill the idea, it might just move it from peaceful speech to violent revolution. As Kennedy said, 'Those that make peaceful revolution impossible will make violent revolution inevitable.'

Respecting each person's right to their own thoughts and beliefs, and their right to express them is critical to a functioning, peaceful society. If we approve suppression of contrarian speech, we promote the oppression of the people speaking. If we approve suppression of speech, we encourage the enforcement of that suppression through violence. No two people share all the same thoughts and opinions, it is impossible that we will all agree on almost any subject at all. If we do not allow people to speak openly and safely; if we promote suppression of speech; we will bring about a more hostile and violent society.

Free speech is essential for a free democracy.

The government is held more accountable when the people are openly and safely able to express their thoughts on politics. People are able to publicize errors, abuses, or corruption only when they are protected by the freedom of speech.

If we give the government the power to selectively control what speech is allowed or appropriate, then we allow the government to have a means to eliminate dissenting or critical opinion of the government. Without freedom of speech, we do not have democratic control of the government.

Freedom of speech makes peaceful political change a real possibility – one that we have seen in our lifetimes. We are able to change our government policy and even our government itself through our democratic process. To be able to choose the best policy, to be able to choose the best government, the people must be able to discuss whatever issues are important to them. If they are not able to openly and safely discuss these issues, they are not able to make the needed changes to government. If that ability to change the government peacefully is taken away, the only means to change the government is then violence.

Freedom of speech is the oxygen of human rights, democracy, and human progress itself. For people in any society to prosper and escape oppressive persecution, all people must be free to have their own thoughts and to express them.

Representative Democracy or Elected Oligarchy?

Even those who live in a true representative democracy have little impact on the laws that govern them. In fact, this system can very easily, and often does, put power into the hands of a select few who rule over the lives of the many. In all reality, the term representative democracy is a misnomer. We elect a small group of people to rule over us without any ability to change the direction of government during that term. A ruling class of a small group is an oligarchy. Therefore, we don't have a democracy at all. It should more accurately be called an 'elected oligarchy'. In an elected oligarchy it is true that the officials are elected. But they form a small class which rules over the people and the people end up having very little control over their laws as a consequence.

Sovereignty is the supreme power or authority over law; it should rest in the hands of the people. It is the will of the majority which must decide the law in all cases; while also respecting and actively protecting the rights and freedoms of the minority. The other side of this spectrum is a dictatorship, where the individual has no power over the laws at all. It is dictated to them by the few people in charge.

Where do we fit on that spectrum in a representative democracy? Are we closer to the power resting in the hands of all the people equally? Or are we closer to the power resting in the hands of the few? Does electing our representatives every four years mean that we are closer to maximum individual sovereignty? Or does it mean that we are closer to power being held in the hands of the few?

In representative democracies we elect short term dictators. Once they are elected they have impunity to enact laws for the duration of that term, even if those laws are heavily opposed by the majority of voters. The only reason a representative has to listen to constituents is the concern of losing an election in the next cycle. That just means they are concerned they won't be the dictators for the four years after that.

Some might object that, even though a few people rule over us, since we choose who our rulers are that we do live in a democracy. They might state that since we can vote on who rules us that we are the ultimate deciders. Even if one accepts that reasoning, it doesn't change that we live under an elected oligarchy. We have a system that also means a small group of voters can control who rules over us. We all have an equal vote, but that doesn't mean that majority opinion wins. Often a minority opinion wins.

We do not have the will of the majority deciding the law in 'first past the post' representative democracies. This can stray very far from the decision making in laws or policies being determined by the majority.

For any political party to hold 100% power over all the provincial laws and policies, they only need one more than

50% of the seats in the government. With the first past the post system, the candidate with the most votes – with a plurality, not a majority – wins. It is not at all uncommon for a candidate to win their seat with 40% of the popular vote in that riding.

This means that it is entirely possible that the 50% of the seats needed to win 100% of the power could be won with the support of only 40% of the people in those ridings. It is also possible that this party would get no significant support in the other ridings. So if the party got 40% support in only 50% of the ridings, and just 5% support in all the others, they can form a majority government despite the fact they only got 23% of the entire popular vote.

This figure gets even worse if we include the percentage of eligible voters that actually voted. It is not uncommon in democracies for only 60%-70% of eligible voters to vote; the rest abstained for whatever reason they chose. That means that in this scenario only 14% of eligible voters are able control 100% of the power in a representative democracy with first past the post elections.

This isn't hypothetical. We have seen times where a minority vote controlled 100% of the power many times in government – often with as little as 40% of the popular vote or 24% of the eligible vote. This illustrates how a minority of voters in a nation can control 100% of the power and are able to enact laws against the wishes of the majority. They are also able to enact those laws against the wishes of the majority because they have a plausible chance of being re-elected with only minority support just like they were the last time.

We only have a say in government during elections.

With a representative democracy, we only have a say in any aspect of government during the election process itself. In between the election cycle, we don't have any say in any law or policy. Our representatives have 100% of the power then.

If we only have a say for a single day once every four years, we really only have control over government 0.068% of the time. Having 0.068% control over government sounds less like the power being held by all the people equally, than by a few. Indeed, with representative democracy we don't choose the laws, we simply choose who rules over us. With the people having no power at all in between election cycles, the truth is we elect four-year term dictators.

The choice of who rules over us is often based on lies.

During the one day, every four years when we actually have any power, our ability to exercise that power is often illusionary as our choices are often presented based on falsehoods. Politicians notoriously will say one thing during the election process and do something entirely different once they are in the government. Or they will enact legislation which was never mentioned during the election process at all.

Both of these mean that the people are in fact not voting for the policies that actually come into play. They were voting for something else that never comes to be because they were misled.

Since they've elected a four-year term dictator, they now have no choice but to accept this until the next election cycle when they will be lied to again and vote for policies that again won't be true. That isn't at all a surprise. The only surprises are that with a system with so little accountability that people expect anything else; and that some people continue to think the solution is to just elect someone else rather than fixing the system itself.

We choose a representative that will never believe everything you believe.

No representative will ever align completely with everything you believe. So you choose representatives based on the best choice – not one which agrees in every case; you might like one policy but dislike others.

That means what you believe for policies in government is only ever partially represented with this system. It is impossible with this system for everything you believe to be reflected in government. This further dilutes the power that the individual has over the law.

With a representative democracy, the individual never has any direct power or influence on a specific law. Even all citizens collectively don't have that power. That power is only in the hands of the few. If every single citizen opposed any specific law or motion they are powerless to stop it or change it. The only recourse to them is the threat of not supporting these representatives during the next election cycle. Given that they are sold policies that are often lies, and given that the government can also get re-elected with minority support, this threat often has no teeth. It is no wonder that historically, that threat has not prevented bad politicians from acting in their own interests, or the interests of their supporters, rather than in the interests of the people.

The people have no direct power over law at all. Not having direct ability to influence the law allows politicians to act in this way. It likely encourages it. Politicians that can use the system will advance higher and higher in station when they can get an unfair advantage to themselves that their honest competitors will not.

In terms of the ability to directly influence law, citizens in a representative democracy have virtually no sovereignty at all. The power is in the hands of the few. Representative democracies are really just elected oligarchies.

First past the post representative democracies give a means for the minority opinion to have 100% power. It means the majority opinion is often ignored. This system keeps the power in the hands of the few. We have no power in choosing the rules; we can only have some power to choose the rulers. But when we are given the option, we are often given lies. Our choice in ruler can never believe everything you believe, so all your beliefs cannot be represented.

This all adds up to the individual having very little control over the laws that govern them. It means that all in all, we do not have any consent of the governed in representative democracies. We have rulers and subjects.

Only tyrants want to dominate people. We are not tyrants and we must never accept stomping on the face of another person to advance our own desires. Egalitarians want to negotiate a compromise approved by the majority while also protecting the individual rights and freedoms of the minority.

Yes, we can vote, but that vote has less influence on actual law and policy than it should. In fact, it has next to none. With first a first past the post representative government, the rule of the majority opinion is in no way guaranteed. Once the government is chosen, there is no ability for a citizen to impact law. We only have a say once every few years during an election, and at that time we are often deceived. Pure representative democracy, especially with a first past the post electoral process, doesn't increase democratic power; it diminishes democratic power.

But that can be changed by introducing a significant measure of direct democratic power to the people.

Use a Deferred Direct Democracy to Maximize Individual Power over Government

In order to have the true benefits of freedom and democracy, the people must have the ultimate and supreme power over the laws. That means that an elected few must not be able to enact laws or policies that disagree with the majority opinion.

How best to do this?

Do we continue to use a representative democracy? As previously shown, the representative democracy is actually a very poor method for bringing about rule by the majority opinion.

Do we change to a direct democracy? Where every decision, law, and policy must be voted upon by the people.

What are the benefits and disadvantages of these two systems?

Representative democracies are cost effective, direct democracies are more expensive.

Having an election once every few years to determine leadership, and then allowing that leadership to govern is a very cost effective method. Elections are not cheap, but nor are they expensive when compared with the usual day to day functions of government.

Whereas direct democracies are much more expensive. An election is required for every single decision. The government can make a few hundred laws in a year. Having each citizen voting on each law would be extremely expensive.

In addition to the cost of running a vote for each motion, the people must take more and more time out of their daily lives which cost them time and money which they could instead be putting towards working, spending time with their family, or leisure. That cost is not insignificant.

Representative democracy allows people who are focused and knowledgeable on the government to govern.

The tasks of government take a great deal of focus and knowledge. Having representatives who are dedicated to that task does help ensure that a thorough consideration is made towards all decisions.

The only issue here is that this can be so easily abused and misused for the benefit of the representative and their associates. Direct democracy, while controlled by people who are not able to dedicate the same focus to public matters, means that the people can bypass partisanship, and bypass political corruption.

People are more politically involved in direct democracies.

A major complaint about representative democracies is that the people often feel that their vote doesn't matter. The party structure holds so much weight and power over the voting process that the outcome feels predetermined. And whomever they elect will just be a part of the system which gets played to the benefit of the political class rather than for the people themselves.

Some might consider these examples to be cynical. But they are legitimate concerns caused by real life examples.

Because direct democracy can bypass partisan loyalty, and because direct democracy means the majority opinion is the deciding factor, the vote of an individual has more meaning, influence, and impact.

This means that fewer people consider their vote to be wasted when it is being directly applied to a specific law.

Direct democracy can ease political fighting.

Another major disadvantage with representative democracy is the political fighting it creates. With representative democracy, especially with a first past the post electoral system, it really is an all or nothing game.

People feel that if their party loses they have no representation at all. Their political preferences are ignored, and they feel that they themselves are ignored.

Direct democracy also eliminates that. People will still disagree on political issues but they can now debate issue by issue, rather than having to dig into positions that are in line with the political party they support, just to ensure they win.

Direct democracy allows a person's nuanced opinions to have power.

With representative democracy, you must choose the party that most closely aligns with your beliefs. But no party will ever match that perfectly. That is simply because no two people alive or dead have ever shared all the same thoughts or beliefs. Likewise, each party will have positions that don't agree with what you think is right.

Because representative politics are an all or nothing game, you must simply pick the party that has the most that is closest to what you hold to be most important and has the least that is farthest.

Direct democracy, on the other hand, offers a means where every political opinion you have can be directly applied to each and every position.

You might agree with a party on policy '1' but disagree on policy '6'. With a representative democracy, you must cede your opinion on policy '6' if you feel that policy '1' is more important. With direct democracy, you can vote exactly as you like for each policy.

We can get most of the benefits of both systems with a hybrid – a Deferred Direct Democracy.

We are not forced to choose only between representative democracy and direct democracy. We can choose a third option that is a hybrid between the two: a representative democracy with strong direct democratic power.

What would this look like?

It is actually not a major change from representative democracy at all. With only a few small adjustments in our law and the democratic process, we can be given ultimate control over all law and policy where each citizen has an equal voice – equal power – in the creation of the law. Then we can have a true rule of the majority opinion. Those adjustments are very simply giving citizens the following powers:

Citizen Initiative – where citizens can propose a motion for a law or policy and, if they are able to get enough popular support as demonstrated by a petition, that motion must be read, debated, and then voted upon in the Legislative Assembly.

Citizen Veto Power via Referendum – If the government votes to pass a motion or bill – or if they vote against a motion or a bill – and enough people disagree, they can force it to a referendum. Then citizens will vote directly on that item and the majority opinion of voters will be the final decider. With Citizen Veto Power, the people are the ultimate deciders in the law.

Recall Legislation – If enough citizens in a riding feel that their representative no longer represents them, they can force that riding to a by-election to vote on the representative again, even if not during a regular election cycle.

With these three powers, the people gain control over their laws. The ultimate power of the law goes out of the hands of the few and into the hands of the people. The minority opinion can never dominate the majority opinion. And each individual can directly affect each law should they choose to.

A differed direct democracy, a hybrid representative democracy with direct democratic powers such as this, isn't a new idea. It has already been done for hundreds of years with great success. Switzerland is an excellent example of a nation where each law is subject to be taken to a referendum if the people wish it. This isn't a new feature in Switzerland, it has been a central focus for hundreds of years to ensure that no people and no party can ever rule over them. They are the final say in each law – if they choose to exercise that power.

Representative democracies offer cost effectiveness, leadership, focus, and knowledge; but they reduce the power of the people, threaten the rule of the majority opinion, and are prone to corruption. Direct democracy gives the people power, reduces corruption, reduces the influence of third parties; but they are more expensive. A deferred direct democracy with strong direct democratic powers means people have the efficiency of representative democracy but have the power of direct democracy on any issue where there is a popular support to exercise that power. Deferred direct democracy is the blueprint for a truly free people.

Citizen Initiative

Imagine that you had a great idea for a new law or a new policy.

Currently, in Alberta and Canada, there is only one method for a citizen to ever get their ideas into the debate in the Legislative Assembly – that is to find an elected Member of the Legislative Assembly who is willing to read your motion in the House.

But perhaps there isn't a single politician who is willing to read your motion. Perhaps your motion would reduce the power of politicians and increase the power of the general public. In that case, most politicians tend to object to such ideas and refuse to support them.

Where does that leave us? If the general public would greatly support such a motion shouldn't they have the power to have it as a possibility in a vote?

We don't have that power right now. There is nothing a citizen can do except stand on a soap box. Simply being able to share an opinion with the public is not enough. The people should have the power to directly bring their ideas into the debate in the Legislative Assembly itself.

Citizen initiatives do not go directly to a vote by referendum; they go directly to the Legislative Assembly where they must be read, debated, and voted upon by the elected representatives.

Initiatives should be treated like any other motion presented in the Legislative Assembly. We want our elected representatives to debate the issue like they would any other motion.

This gives many advantages over sending initiatives directly to a referendum instead of to the legislature.

Firstly, it is more cost effective. Referendums are more expensive than representative democracy. Referendums should be limited to where there is significant public disagreement to the government decisions. It shouldn't be the standard method of legislation.

Secondly, it forces the debate to include people who are focused on legislation. The average citizen is unable to devote the same amount of time and focus on the government that an elected representative can. This doesn't mean the citizen is less intelligent. It is simply that they have a career they must devote time to which isn't politics. Conversely, the representative's career is politics. This means they are likely to have an insight which should be included in these issues.

Lastly, this method allows the debate that was in the House to be on the public record so that citizens can review that debate for maximum insight on the issue. They can then throw their support either for or against it.

A citizen initiative must have significant popular support before it can be sent to the Legislative Assembly.

We obviously don't want a single citizen to be able to force every idea they have to a vote where there isn't obvious popular support for that idea. If we did, we are guaranteed to be inundated with thousands or perhaps hundreds of thousands of ridiculous and unpopular ideas that do nothing more than waste time and money.

We don't want crazy or prank ideas dominating the time, energy, and resources of our legislature. We want to keep initiatives to those that obviously enjoy significant popular support.

We also want citizens to have real and meaningful ability to exercise their right of initiative.

The process cannot be so arduous that it becomes practically impossible for it to ever be used. It must be at a level where a group of people can reasonably work without great sacrifice of time or money.

It should also be at a level where just two citizens could work full time over the span of the allotted timeframe to achieve the petition.

Petitions supporting an initiative should have a long enough period to be able to spread the idea but not be so long as to be in effect indefinitely.

A petition that can last forever will be able to get enough signatures or support even if there isn't true popular support behind the motion. Therefore we need to have a time limit allocated to each petition.

But that limit should be very generous in length to maximize the ability of supporters to spread the idea to fellow citizens and to gather more support in favour of their motion.

A time limit of 18 months is a reasonable limit to the time required to demonstrate support for a motion. Going with the concept that on the extreme end two individuals should have the power to achieve this if they devoted themselves to it full time, we have a method of deciding how many people should support this motion. On average, a person canvassing door to door is able to get 10 signatures per hour on a reasonably popular position. So two people devoting themselves full time can expect to get about 60,000 signatures in an 18-month span.

If they are able to get people that are also helping then it becomes much easier. With 10 people helping each person must devote one day per week. With 80 people that gets reduced to one hour per week. With 400 people it becomes one hour per week for only 15 weeks.

This is a limit that is both high enough to reduce the risk of unpopular motions wasting time in the legislature, but low enough that many people can reasonably achieve it; and on the extreme end, a single person can as well if they devoted themselves to it full time.

To start the petition process, at least two citizens must support that the motion should be debated in the legislature.

Having more than one person required just to start the process of a petition is used to prevent time and money being wasted on a process that is only supported by one single person.

Multiple methods should be included in determining popular support for any initiative.

We want a multiple of options available to citizens to be able to participate in a petition.

Citizens can take their petition and canvass with it.

A copy of the petition should be kept at select Government administrative buildings where citizens can also go to sign to show their support.

In addition, we can go even further than that and allow citizens to voice their support without meeting anyone else who does in person. In the electronic age, this should not be difficult.

By using electronic methods, citizens can use social media to help spread their idea and to get support that their idea should be debated in the legislature.

To support a petition, citizens should be able to send a simple text message to an automated system. There they can submit their name and all other pertinent information. The phone number will have to match the name of the citizen, which must also be cross-referenced with a list of eligible voters.

Additionally, an insignificant, tax deductible fee of perhaps $0.50 can be charged to the person's phone bill. This provides a means of confirmation and double checking against fraud. If a person didn't support this motion, they can discover that their phone was used against their wishes on their monthly bill, and can then contend their inclusion in the petition.

Likewise, we can use the internet to make this an easier and cost effective system. A government website can accept online support. To prevent abuse, like above, we would need a reasonable method of verification. A person would have to put in their name and address – which would be cross-referenced to a list of eligible voters. In addition, they would have to pay a tax deductible $0.50 fee with a credit card that matches the name and address.

Like above, that transaction isn't just used as verification of identity, but it provides another cross check. If a citizen sees a charge where they didn't support the petition, they are made aware of it on their monthly bill and can contend it.

Some people might object to the inclusion of electronic methods in demonstrating support for petitions. Electronic means are susceptible to being hacked. This method has a few safeguards in place to reduce that threat. It uses a government system with the appropriate level of internet security and internet security staff. It uses infrastructure already in place attached to a name and address that is used daily – phone numbers, and credit cards. We can require a citizen to pre-register with ID to verify electronic methods prior to their use.

Electronic support of a petition can be spot checked, exactly like signatures on petitions must be spot checked to ensure they are valid.

Additionally, these electronic methods are never used to actually vote on the law. All they do is demonstrate support for a petition for a motion to be read, debated, and then voted upon by the Legislative Assembly. If they were successfully hacked, then all that would do is force a motion to a vote in the House. The hacking couldn't prevent a citizen initiative because only 'yes' votes are counted. It is assumed that there isn't enough popular support for a citizen initiative until that support is demonstrated; and only if enough 'yes' votes for the initiative are counted does it need to be presented to the Legislative Assembly. People can't vote against the petition except by not signing and supporting it.

Electronic methods to demonstrate support are no more risky than signatures on written petitions. Electronic support - where there are reasonable effort and security to ensure there isn't double voting and to ensure voting is of citizens only - cannot usurp the power of citizen initiative.

Citizens can still get an elected representative to read their motion on their behalf if that representative chooses to.

Citizen Initiative isn't meant to eliminate the ability of a citizen to approach an elected representative to support their motion.

That would be the easiest method to get a motion debated in the Legislative Assembly and should be the first method used by a citizen.

Citizen initiative is designed to provide a means where citizens can bypass politicians if none will support their idea. It is designed to allow citizens a means to directly propose laws and policies when they have sufficient popular support from their fellow citizens.

A successful citizen initiative petition is no guarantee that it will be successful in the Legislative Assembly.

Not every motion or bill debated in the legislature will be supported by the majority of representatives. That is true of motions presented by the elected representatives themselves. We can expect it to also be true of motions presented by citizens.

Simply because a citizen is successful in getting enough popular support to have a motion read does not mean that the motion will become law or policy. It might very well be voted down in the legislature.

If the Legislative Assembly rejects the motion, citizens are still able to work for it to become law.

Even if the legislature votes down the motion, that is not the end for the citizen. If they choose, they can work to get enough popular support to force the motion to a referendum. If that is successful, then all citizens will be able to directly vote on this issue and the decision of the majority will be the law or policy.

Citizen initiative removes the monopoly of power over ideas of policy from the hands of a few and gives that power equally to all citizens. New and innovative ideas can come from anyone, and we want those ideas to have an ability to be seriously considered if they are able to get enough popular support to merit that consideration.

Citizen Veto Power via Referendum: Ultimate Power over Government is Equally in the Hands of the Individual Citizens

On most motions or bills, so long as the representatives are properly representing the people who have elected them, there won't be much need for a referendum. All decisions by the government are assumed to be accepted by the majority of citizens unless a sufficient portion demonstrates their disapproval by petitioning for a referendum on it.

But there will be times when the representative government is outside of the sphere of the majority opinion. In those times we don't want the government to be able to bring about legislation against the will of the majority opinion. We want the people to have the final say in any government decision.

Citizen Veto Power via Referendum moves the power from the hands of a few into the hands of all citizens.

With pure representative democracy, the citizens don't have the highest power at all. That rests with the elected representatives. Effectively, citizens vote for their rulers, but they are still ruled.

Citizen Veto Power via Referendum changes that dynamic. The people are not ruled in this case. Each and every law must be accepted by the majority of people to be valid. The majority of people must consent to be governed by these laws or the law can be eliminated.

That puts the final say not in the hands of a few people, but in the hands of all people equally.

Any decision made by the government can be forced to a referendum.

The power of citizen veto is not limited to laws or policies the government passes. It can be applied to laws or policies the government rejects as well.

If the government passes a law or policy where there is sufficient disagreement then that can be forced to a referendum. That way the government cannot pass anything against the wishes of the majority opinion.

Likewise, if the government rejects a motion, the people should be able to bypass them and vote directly on it themselves.

This means that the budget can be forced to a referendum if the citizens object to going into a deficit.

Citizen Veto Power via Referendum doesn't need to be used on each and every law.

Direct democracies are expensive because each law, and every other decision of government must be voted on by each citizen. That is a long, arduous, and costly process.

Citizen Veto Power keeps the same power in the hands of the people but doesn't share the same cost. This is simply because most laws shouldn't need to have a referendum. And indeed, so long as the representatives' decisions are closely aligned with the majority opinion, they won't.

Referendums are only utilized when there is enough disagreement with the government decision to warrant bringing the matter to a referendum. When a government passes a law or motion which the vast majority accept, then there is no need for a referendum. The law is shown to be accepted because the people did not exercise their power of veto. When there is enough discontentment with any law, the people are able to force it to a referendum, where all people will vote directly on that law.

We want opposition to government decisions demonstrated quickly.

We don't want to have government decisions stuck in limbo for all time, otherwise they will be unable to act decisively when needed. Other actors, such as businesses or other governments, will be unsure of the direction or strength of law if laws can be reversed at any time for whatever reason.

Any government decision should have a 100-day delay before coming into effect with a few exceptions for emergencies. The citizenry has until that 100 days expires to demonstrate that the law is contentious enough to warrant a referendum on the decision.

This gives the citizens real ability to make a change but gives a set time limit so citizens and other third party actors know what decision has been made and when it comes into effect.

To start a the petition for a referendum we need to show real support for it.

We should require 100 people to sponsor the referendum initiative and they should pay a deposit.

We want 100 people because we don't even want this to be able to be started with just one or two people; there needs to be a sign of support right from the beginning. Otherwise, all our laws might have opposition and petitions to reverse them.

Getting 100 sponsors means a significant support from the start, while not being so onerous that this level of support couldn't be gathered by just a single person in a reasonable time frame.

The deposit must be equal 1/3 of the hourly minimum wage per sponsor. In 2018, the minimum hourly wage in Alberta will be $15. So 1/3 of that is $5. The deposit required will then be $500. This is not an undue hardship for each sponsor to provide.

Requiring a $500 deposit also reduces the risk of abuse because it has a real cost to the people. If the petition for a referendum is successful, then the $500 deposit is returned. This is because the deposit is there to dissuade frivolous attempts at referendums, not to dissuade actually exercising the power of the people.

Having a deposit makes sense to reduce abuse. But having a large amount reduces democratic power to only the very wealthy. That isn't the point here.

Having a deposit rather than a fee also makes sense. The point is to reduce abuse, not to finance the process. The democratic process is paid by taxes of all citizens because it is enjoyed by all citizens. We don't want fees for people exercising their democratic rights.

We don't want good laws or good government decisions being forced to a referendum frivolously.

A referendum can only be forced when there is demonstrable popular support for the referendum. We don't want a hand full of people to be able to force a referendum. Otherwise, we know that every decision will be sent to a referendum and we will have a legislative system bogged down by redundant procedure and wasted resources. A petition showing that there is significant popular support must be completed.

We want regulations that make forcing a referendum a practically possible option for citizens.

There is a balance that we require for this to be effective. If we require too little popular support demonstrated in a petition, we waste time and resources with too many referendums. If we require too much popular support, then Citizen Veto Power loses its strength as it is never able to be practically put into effect.

The number of signatures required on a petition must:

1. Be substantial enough to prevent frivolous referendums

2. Be small enough for citizens to achieve

3. Reflect the size of the voting population at any given time.

The petition should, therefore, require signatures equaling at least 5% of the number of citizens who voted during the last general election.

In Alberta during the 2015 election, approximately 2.5 million people voted. That would mean that we would require 125,000 citizens supporting a petition for a referendum.

This is a very large number that reduces the risk of frivolous abuse. But it is also a number that is demonstrated as being possible. In Alberta, a recent petition with over 160,000 signatures was delivered to the Legislative Assembly. Unfortunately for the supporters of this petition, there was no power of petition or referendum in Alberta or Canada, so it didn't have to be enforced, debated, read or even acknowledged by the government.

This would change that. That effort, and the people who supported it, would actually have had the power to force the motion they rejected to a referendum where all citizens could equally vote on it.

We want to make the process easy enough to succeed when enough people support it.

The point of the number of signatures isn't to make it difficult for people who disagree with the government, but to show that enough people agree that it should be decided by referendum instead of by a few representatives. As such we want to keep the required number of supporters high, but we want to have measures to make it easy for a citizen to validly support the petition.

The typical method for getting petitions signed is for canvassers to walk home by home and knock on their doors asking for signatures. This is a very time-consuming process. It is how the petition for 160,000 signatures was achieved, so it is possible, but it isn't in any way easy.

Using electronic methods which cross reference voters, use registered verifications, and use third party verification such as cell phone numbers and credit cards is a method to increase citizen participation. The same methods suggested in the chapter for citizen initiatives can be applied here as well.

Some people might object to the inclusion of electronic methods in demonstrating support for petitions. Electronic means are susceptible to being hacked. This method has a few safeguards in place to reduce that threat. It uses a government system with the appropriate level of internet security and internet security staff. It uses infrastructure already in place attached to a name and address that is used daily – phone numbers, and credit cards. We can require a citizen to pre-register with ID to verify electronic methods prior to their use.

Additionally, these electronic methods are never used to actually vote on the law. All they do is demonstrate support for a petition for a law or government decision to go to a referendum rather than be decided by representatives. If they were successfully hacked, then all that would do is force a motion to a referendum where the people decide directly. The hacking couldn't prevent a citizen veto because only 'yes' votes are counted. It is assumed all citizens accept a motion, and only if enough 'yes' votes for a referendum are counted does the referendum take place. People can't vote against the petition except by not signing and supporting it.

So electronic support where there are reasonable effort and security to ensure there isn't double voting and to ensure voting is of citizens only cannot usurp the veto power of citizens.

Like all laws passed by the government, laws passed by referendum must be constitutionally valid.

Laws passed via referendum are not free from the constitution. In order to be valid, the laws passed must not be unconstitutional.

Laws which are passed in a referendum must not be able to infringe on any citizen's rights and freedoms. Those freedoms are constitutionally protected for the very purpose of preventing laws of every having the ability to remove them in the future.

This prevents mob rule or a dictatorship of the majority. This prevents a majority being able to take away the rights of a minority by means of a referendum.

Referendums can be all grouped together to take place once a year.

People don't want to go to the voting booth every month. And it would also be very expensive to have a referendum every month as well.

Some years there may not be any issues where the citizens think it is either disagreeable or significant enough to bother forcing it to a referendum. During those years, there won't be any cost to a referendum at all.

If in any year there are decisions that the citizens think should be decided by referendum rather than by the representatives, then those referendums can all take place at the same time. People can vote directly on whatever number of referendums are presented at the same time to save both themselves and the government time and money.

Sometimes the people may want to have the referendum right away rather than wait until the next scheduled election date. That decision can also be included in the referendum petition.

This is similar to Switzerland where referendums are grouped together. Their referendums are grouped together and voted on every four months or so. In a democracy where they have had direct power over law for centuries, about a dozen laws are decided by the people directly each year.

Fewer dates for referendums means more savings. More dates for referendums means the decision is made faster. Having the dates set for once a year, but allowing people to bypass that with a faster decision gives the best of both options. It keeps costs lower typically but allows more urgent decisions to be made faster.

Unlike in Canada, no one rules over the Swiss. Their representatives cannot pass laws against the will of the majority of voters. They are in charge of their own laws, their own policies, their own government, and their own lives.

By having a right to any decision made by the government being able to be forced to a referendum; Citizen Veto Power via Referendum moves the power from the few into the hands of all citizens equally. While this right extends to any government decision, Citizen Veto Power via Referendum doesn't need to be used on each and every law. It is only used when the people want it to be used. With the proper process, we reduce the risk of frivolous referendums, but continue to keep that power in the hands of citizens should they need it. With Citizen Veto Power via Referendum, the people are the ultimate and supreme power in government, not the elected representatives; the people are no longer ruled, they are only then truly the rulers.

Recall Legislation

The idea that politicians lie to citizens during the election period in order to be elected certainly isn't new or in any way surprising. What is surprising is that citizens have allowed a system that doesn't give them any recourse at all for so long.

Recall legislation means that an elected representative is not guaranteed their seat for the entire term in between election cycles. With support from a sufficient number of citizens within a riding, the citizens can force that seat to a by-election before the end of their original term. Recall legislation differs from impeachment in that impeachment is a legal process, whereas recall is a political device.

This isn't for vindictiveness, and it isn't due to any anti-politician spirit. There are many reasons that citizens should insist on having recall legislation.

Sometimes a politician is not honest during the election process.

This happens so frequently that many people assume it happens in each and every election with each and every politician. That isn't so, there are good politicians who are honestly working to have good laws and good government for themselves and their neighbours.

But it also happens when a politician will flat out and directly say one thing during the election, but then ignore their own promise once they have power.

Another type of dishonesty is being elected under one public mandate, but then enacting significant laws or policies which were not included in that mandate at all. When a government is elected with a public mandate, but then enacts a law that was not discussed there is no way that the people honestly voted for those different changes.

A politician wins a seat due to vote splitting, but is actually the least favoured option for the majority of people in that riding.

With a first past the post system it is possible for a politician to win their seat with only 30% - 40% support in a riding due to vote splitting.

Sometimes this really isn't too much of an issue. But sometimes the winning party is not only not supported by the majority of people, but that party might be the least desired choice of the majority.

This is a flaw with the first past the post system. It allows a winner to be the one that is the last choice of the majority. That is about as far from the rule of the majority opinion as possible. It takes us away from the power being in the hands of the people and right back into the hands of the few.

Your elected representative was honest during the campaign, but no longer represents what you want.

Even where there was no dishonesty in the last election cycle, there can be very significant reasons to implement a recall.

People and situations change. It might be that a representative changed and no longer reflects the will of their constituents. It might be the people changed and no longer want the same representative.

It might just be that the circumstances in the world changed and that representative is no longer the best option.

Each of these are valid reasons for recall. Recall means that the representative is ultimately the best choice for the people at all times, not just for one day every four years.

You sometimes elect a politician based on their membership to one party, then they cross the floor to join a party you don't support.

As of now, there is no recourse for voters when their elected representative abandons the party they were elected under and joins another party.

If they were elected based on their membership to a party that their constituency supports, this effectively means that the voters just lost their vote for the next few years.

Recall legislation means that if the voters still support their representative, there is no need for any action. But if they don't support their representative now that they are no longer part of the same party, they are able to take active steps to get their vote to have meaning again.

We don't want frivolous recall by-elections.

Recall is a power that we want the people to have. But we don't want it to be a power that can be abused by a few people.

Every politician will have political opponents, and very often many of them will be very petty and willing to cause great disruption. This is what we want to avoid.

The recall process must not be able to happen with just a few people. It must take a reasonably sufficient popular support.

What have other governments done? Has it been successful in giving recall powers to the people? Has it caused excessive abuse and inefficient elections?

Look at British Columbia to see what not to do.

British Columbia instituted recall legislation in 1991.

Since then there have been 26 attempts at recall, but not a single one was successful. This isn't because the recall attempts were frivolous. Indeed, two of the politicians where this was attempted were so unpopular that they shortly resigned on their own – but they weren't required to.

The recall legislation failed to give the citizens the direct power to remove those very unpopular politicians.

This is because the recall legislation in place in BC is set to a level where while they have recall legislation, the means are too strict to ever be able to actually happen. Impossible laws are as bad as not having them in the first place.

In BC, 40% of all registered voters must sign a petition in favour of a recall election. That might not seem like it is too high until we examine how many people even bother to vote. That number has been as low as 40% and rarely goes above 60%. This means that in order for a recall election to take place we require between 67% and 100% of actual voters to agree.

Once we have those numbers, we see immediately why that is impossible to ever actually happen.

Using 40% of the registered voters – which means using between 67% and 100% of actual voters - has failed to demonstrate that the people have an effective method of recall.

What can we learn from British Columbia's recall legislation?

Base the requirements of signatures mainly on a percentage of voter turnout in the last election.

Having the requirements based on the actual voter turnout has many benefits. Firstly, it means that recall efforts are based on current political engagement. If the public is generally not engaged and is abstaining from politics, we don't want that abstention to prevent politically active citizens from being able to exercise their rights and power.

It also has a practical benefit. If only 20% of the registered voters bothered to vote in the last election which won the representative their seat, and they only need a plurality of those votes, then why would we want 40% of the people to be required to vote against that candidate for a by-election?

Stick with a rule of majority.

Favouring majority opinion is a strong element of a democracy and should be considered whenever possible. It shows the desire for the will of the people to be realized. It means we want the most people as possible to have the laws they want.

By following the last two policies of basing the required signatures on a percentage of voter turnout, and sticking with a rule of majority, we come to a good compromise. We need 50% of the number of voters in the last election to support a recall election. This percentage is slightly higher than is found in Kansas, where they require 40% of the number of people that voted in the last election. Kansas has not had frivolous elections; but, unlike British Columbia, has had successful recall elections to remove representatives who are no longer wanted by the majority of people.

To start a recall election we need to show real support for it.

We should require 100 people to sponsor the recall initiative and they should pay a deposit.

We want 100 people because we don't even want this to be able to be started with just one or two people. Otherwise, all our ridings will be in a state of perpetual recall attempts because there will be people trying to oust their representatives.

Getting 100 sponsors means a significant support from the start, while not being so onerous that this level of support couldn't be gathered by just a single person in a reasonable time frame.

The deposit must be equal 1/3 of the hourly minimum wage per sponsor. In 2018, the minimum hourly wage in Alberta will be $15. So 1/3 of that is $5. The deposit required will then be $500. This is not an undue hardship for each sponsor to provide.

Requiring a $500 deposit also reduces the risk of abuse because it has a real cost to the people. If the recall is successful, then the $500 deposit is returned. This is because the deposit is there to dissuade frivolous attempts at referendums, not to dissuade actually exercising the power of the people.

Having a deposit makes sense to reduce abuse. But having a large amount reduces democratic power to only the very wealthy. That isn't the point here.

Having a deposit rather than a fee also makes sense. The point is to reduce abuse, not to finance the process. The democratic process is paid by taxes of all citizens because it is enjoyed by all citizens. We don't want fees for people exercising their democratic rights.

To force the by-election a petition based on a majority of the voter turnout in the election that won the representative their seat is required.

The number of people required to sign a petition in support of the recall legislation should be equal to 50% of the voter turnout.

Some people might think this number is too low, and that it will cause frequent and consistent recall by-elections. But that isn't the case. The US State of Michigan has had recall legislation since 1908. They only require 25% of the voters in the last election to bring about another election.

Despite having a much smaller requirement than proposed here, they have only had 5 successful recalls – two Mayors, two Senators, and one State Representative.

This is a requirement which does not expose itself to abuse but shows that it can actually work.

Requiring a majority rather than 25% is to reflect that the majority opinion is preferred.

Use multiple methods to sign the petition.

Just like with the citizen power of initiative, we want to use electronic methods to increase citizen engagement.

Citizens can take their petition and canvass with it.

A copy of the petition should be kept at select Government administrative buildings where citizens can also go to sign to show their support.

Electronic methods using text messages and the internet can be included. By using electronic methods, citizens can use social media to help spread their idea and to get support for their recall initiative.

Using text messages is viable and is as reasonably secure and verifiable as signatures are. With text messages, citizens can submit their name and all other pertinent information. The phone number will have to match the name of the citizen, which must also be cross-referenced with a list of eligible voters.

Additionally, an insignificant, tax deductible fee of perhaps $0.50 can be charged to the person's phone bill. This provides a means of confirmation and double checking against fraud. If a person didn't support this motion, they can discover that their phone was used against their wishes on their monthly bill, and can then contend their inclusion in the petition.

Likewise, we can use the internet to make this an easier and cost effective system. A government website can accept online support. To prevent abuse, like above, we would need a reasonable method of verification. A person would have to put in their name and address – which would be cross-referenced to a list of eligible voters. In addition, they would have to pay a tax deductible $0.50 fee with a credit card that matches the name and address.

Like above, that transaction isn't just used as verification of identity, but it provides another cross check. If a citizen sees a charge where they didn't support the petition, they are made aware of it on their monthly bill and can contend it.

Some people might object to the inclusion of electronic methods in demonstrating support for petitions. Electronic means are susceptible to being hacked. This method has a few safeguards in place to reduce that threat. It uses a government system with the appropriate level of internet security and internet security staff. It uses infrastructure already in place attached to a name and address that is used daily – phone numbers, and credit cards. We can require a citizen to pre-register with ID to verify electronic methods prior to their use.

Electronic support of a petition can be spot checked, exactly like signatures on petitions must be spot checked to ensure they are valid. Electronic methods to demonstrate support are no more risky than signatures on written petitions. Electronic support - where there are reasonable effort and security to ensure there isn't double voting and to ensure voting is of citizens only – cannot deny citizens the suffrage to vote for their chosen representative.

Additionally, these electronic methods are never used to actually vote for a representative. All they do is demonstrate support for a new election. The election itself should not have any electronic methods. It should be simple paper with multiple checks and balances.

We don't want by-elections immediately after the last or before the next election.

We don't want to have by-elections that would be wasteful of money if we either just had an election or because another election is coming up.

If a candidate just won an election, we want to minimize any threat of an immediate and unnecessary backlash from their political opponents. The candidate won, let's give them a chance to do their job.

Likewise, what is the point of a by-election if there is another general election just around the corner? There isn't much point in wasting time and money for an election that will only give a short term before yet another election. We might as well deal with any concerns at the next scheduled election.

On the other hand, it is possible to learn that a politician was just the absolute worst choice and should be removed. We don't want to remove that power from citizens, but we also want to reduce that waste.

The solution is to allow recall at any time but to make it more difficult immediately after or before elections.

While recall petitions should normally require support equaling 50% of the voter turnout in the last election; within 12 months of the last or next election, a petition must require the support of 50% of the eligible voters in the riding.

This has many significant factors.

Firstly, it respects the will of the majority at all times. If the absolute majority of eligible voters have a desire for a new by-election then that should be respected and obeyed.

Secondly, it is very difficult to achieve and is therefore unlikely to ever actually happen. BC has been unable to ever get a by-election when they require 40% of the eligible voters to support it. 50% is even more difficult.

This means that we will eliminate frivolous recall attempts but the possibility is still there in the event of a massive dissatisfaction of the majority of voters with their representative.

A successful recall petition doesn't mean the representative must leave their seat.

A successful recall only means that there must be a by-election. It doesn't mean that the representative will lose that by-election.

That representative is allowed to run as a candidate again. They might just win again as well.

Given that a by-election requires 50% support of the number of voters in the last election it is very unlikely that the representative would win again, but it is still possible. Even though 50% disapprove of the candidate, that 50% might split their vote which could allow the candidate to win again. More people might show up to vote in support of the candidate and they might even get a majority.

The petition doesn't control who is elected. It only controls if there is a by-election or not. The people's vote determines who will be the elected representative, not a petition.

Recall legislation means that the people can rectify a bad choice or a choice that is no longer appropriate. It reduces the threat of a representative acting against the public interest. It increases the democratic power of the people because they have the potential for a vote at all times and not just once every four years.

Laws Should Be Created, Controlled, and Enforced as Locally as Is Practical.

Every person should have as much control over the laws that directly affect their lives as possible. They shouldn't control the laws that affect other people's lives, and not their own.

The only way to achieve this is local control over the law. That goes against the most common paradigm of nation states right now. Most western democracies evolved slowly from monarchies. They mimic the control that a central monarch had over the land. This system minimizes the democratic power that citizens have in it.

With a central power, each person's vote has less direct impact on the laws that affect themselves, and more impact on the laws that affect other people's lives. This is the opposite of what we want in an ethical democratic system.

But if laws were controlled more locally, then each person would have more control over the laws that govern themselves, and less control over the laws that govern other people.

The laws of one local area do not affect people that don't live there. The laws in France don't affect people who live in

Russia. Therefore, only people in France should have any say in the laws in France. People in Russia should have no say at all in them.

That concept can be applied in Canada to the provinces. The laws in Alberta do not affect people that don't live here. And likewise, the laws outside of Alberta don't affect the people that live in Alberta. So only Albertans should control the laws in Alberta – which means they will have 10 times the democratic power over their laws than they currently do. And Albertans should not have any say at all in the laws outside of Alberta – meaning they will not be controlling the laws that affect other people's lives but not their own.

That would be the justest system.

In most cases, the laws will actually be very similar. That is the case all over the world. We don't expect to go anywhere on Earth where murder is not against the law.

In democracies, these laws also tend to be very similar. When a person from Canada goes to Germany, they don't expect massive or significant differences in law. And indeed, there aren't many. People from different free nations with different laws can visit each other without much problem.

Really, there are only three possible outcomes if Albertans had complete control over their laws:

1. The laws would be exactly the same as it is in the rest of Canada.

2. The laws would be only slightly different reflecting a nuanced difference in the population.

3. The laws would be entirely different.

Where the laws would be the same, there isn't an issue.

Where the people want the laws to be slightly different to reflect their own nuanced approach, the laws should be slightly different.

Where the people want the laws to be very different, it is obvious that this local area has a dramatic difference of opinion on that matter. The laws should reflect that difference with the local thought on the subject.

As an example, let's imagine that Albertans wanted to change the law dealing with grand theft. In Canada, at the time of this writing, grand theft is theft of property greater than $5000 in value.

Perhaps Albertans think that number is too low and it is causing too many people to go to jail for too long a time than is worth the crime. After all, a $5000 theft in Canada can get a person ten years in jail. Perhaps Albertans think ten years of a person's life is too strict for $5000. Perhaps they want it raised. Perhaps they want to add a new section of theft between $5000 and $20,000, and then have theft greater than $20,000 be the most severe. If we did this, we'd save far more than $5000 in jailing costs. So there is logic to this.

But, as shown above, Albertans have no power to make this change. It's what they would want but their vote is effectively meaningless in Ottawa.

Now if we had local control, we could do this. Albertans could change the punishment for theft to help a person who made a mistake get back on their feet and be a productive member of society, and also save hundreds of thousands of dollars in jail costs.

Or let's imagine that Albertans want theft under $100 to not have a criminal record for the first or second offense. They want it to be punished, but perhaps only with community service so we don't waste tens of thousands on a crime that cost $90. Perhaps they wouldn't want the crime to have a criminal record because they don't want a person to lose the ability to have a job because they made a stupid mistake and it is too trivial to ruin a person's prospects for life.

What would be the problem for that in Quebec? Does it change anything in Quebec or Ontario? No. They still have the theft laws exactly as they want them. But now Albertans have them as they want them as well. Locally sovereign governments mean more democracy.

All people should have as much democratic control over the laws that govern their lives as is reasonably possible. If a democracy is spread over large geographies with large populations, then the individual's vote is diluted. Only with local control of Government can the ideal of individuals having optimal control over the laws that govern their lives ever be realized.

Localism Doesn't Mean Left Wing or Right Wing Politics

Both areas that favour more government spending on social programs and those that favour less have also favoured local government control in the past. This is because the concept of localism doesn't favour any side of the political spectrum. But it does favour all people getting the type of government they want.

If people want to have a social program, but the centralized government is against that program, then the program will be squashed.

Having local control over all laws, however, means that the people in any area are not threatened by the wills of other people that don't live there dominating their political and legal systems. Localism means more people get the government they want.

If we had a government that controlled only two distinct areas, and the majority of people living in Area A want one more social spending by the government, but the majority of people living in Area B want less, then there are only a few possibilities. Either the policy of one area will dominate the other due to having a larger population, or a medial position will be taken.

Neither of those positions is particularly good for everyone.

If one area is able to dominate another, then we have a significant portion of the public living under laws and policies that they dislike. That is true if they favour more government intervention or less. And no people should act to dominate others. If people in an area where you don't live want more government, that doesn't affect you. You shouldn't dominate their wishes on the basis of having a larger population and then cheerfully state how 'democratic' that was because it was majority rule.

Domination of policy is certainly not the solution, but neither is a medial position.

A medial position taken might work if it comes via debate and examination that a middle ground can satisfy everyone's objectives. If that is the case, then it means that the majority change their position to that new middle ground.

But often the medial position doesn't mean that the desired policies of the people have changed. Rather it means that in order to move forward politically a watered down version of each interest is accepted as a compromise. Rather than the majority of each area getting as close to what they want as possible, no one is getting precisely what they want. Everyone is getting a policy that is substandard to everyone in terms of meeting their objections. Really it means a bad policy that no one really likes and very often doesn't actually do anything positive. All that kind of a policy can do is waste money.

The best solution is for Area A to have the policy the majority there want and for Area B to have the policy the majority there want. In that situation, more people have exactly the policy they want. The policy in Area A doesn't affect the people in Area B, and vice versa. That is the optimal solution.

The goal of not being dominated and not dominating others shouldn't be treated as a partisan issue. Freedom, which is to say not being dominated and also not dominating others, is the only moral position to take in government.

Localism means all people get more power to have the policies they want. Whether those policies mean more or fewer government programs isn't an issue with localism. Localism doesn't inhibit people from having more government programs or fewer. It only means that the people living in any given location have more ability to choose the level that they want for themselves.

Localism Means More People Get the Government They Want

With a centralized government, even when it is a democracy, fewer people will have the government they want. Having a vote won't change this. Large geographies make for weak democracies.

A representative democracy is really nothing more than an elected oligarchy. With this type of system it is very easy for only 25% of the people to have 100% control over all laws, taxes, finances, and policies. Then we'd have up to 75% of the people being unhappy with the government, and who could blame them?

On the other hand, the more locally controlled a government is, the more people will be happy with the law. That means more civil behavior.

Let's imagine a nation that has three major population areas. One of those population areas has a million people, the other has two million, and the last has three million. It might seem rather balanced, the two smaller populations equal the one larger one.

What happens when those populations want different laws or policies? How many people will be happy with the laws if they are applied to everyone rather than each population having their own local control over government?

For this, let's consider three scenarios.

Scenario 1:

A policy is heavily favoured in one population, but heavily opposed by the others. The largest population is in favour and the smaller ones are opposed.

	Population 1	Population 2	Population 3
Population	1,000,000	2,000,000	3,000,000
In Favour	287,628(29%)	456,458(23%)	2,578,687(86%)
Against	712,372(71%)	1,543,542(77%)	421,313(14%)
Motion	Passed	Passed	Passed
% Happy	29%	23%	86%

In this case, the motion passes with 55% support. 55% of the total population is happy with the results and what the policy will be. That seems like a triumph of democracy but it actually means that more people are unhappy with the law than need be.

What would this look like if instead of an overarching, centralized government each population instead had control of the laws and policies in their population, and had no control of the laws and policies of people living in other population centers?

In that case, we'd have it look like this:

	Population 1	Population 2	Population 3
Population	1,000,000	2,000,000	3,000,000
In Favour	287,628(29%)	456,458(23%)	2,578,687(86%)
Against	712,372(71%)	1,543,542(77%)	421,313(14%)
Motion	Failed	Failed	Passed
% Happy	71%	77%	86%

Suddenly the majority of people in each and every population center got exactly the policy the majority of people living there wanted.

And collectively more people have the laws and policies they want as well. Instead of having a 55% contentment rate with the laws, 81% of the people are happy with the laws and policies that will govern over their lives.

Scenario 2:

Some people might consider Scenario 1 to be skewed because it was such a divisive policy between each population center. So let's make it less polarized and more evenly spread amongst each population and see if more people will still be happy.

In this scenario, a policy is rather evenly supported down the middle. There are regional differences on the opinion of the policy, but it remains split. The largest population is in favour, but only slightly in the majority. The smaller ones are more against, but again only slightly in the majority.

	Population 1	Population 2	Population 3
Population	1,000,000	2,000,000	3,000,000
In Favour	487,628(49%)	956,458(48%)	1,578,687(53%)
Against	512,372(51%)	1,043,542(52%)	1,421,313(47%)
Motion	Passed	Passed	Passed
% Happy	49%	48%	53%

In this case, the motion carries with 50.4% total support. 50.4% of people got the policy they wanted, and 49.6% of people got a policy they didn't want. 50.4% of the people are happy with the results.

What if each population got the policy of the majority in that population? Then instead of everyone getting the policy, populations 1 and 2 wouldn't have it, but population 3 would.

	Population 1	Population 2	Population 3
Population	1,000,000	2,000,000	3,000,000
In Favour	487,628(49%)	956,458(48%)	1,578,687(53%)
Against	512,372(51%)	1,043,542(52%)	1,421,313(47%)
Motion	Failed	Failed	Passed
% Happy	49%	48%	53%

If that happened, instead of 51% of people in population 1 being unhappy with the vote, only 49% would. Instead of 52% of the people in population 2 being unhappy, only 48% would be.

Overall this means that across all three populations 52% of the people are happy with the results. That's an overall increase of 2% of citizens having the law that they want, even on an issue which is very evenly split among all populations.

This might not seem like much of an increase, but we're talking about a very evenly supported policy. And even if it is small, it is still an increase in laws reflecting the will of the majority.

The fact is there is never a situation where a large, overarching, centralized government can have more citizen contentment with the law than can be achieved with local government control. The absolute best a centralized government can ever do is to equal the contentment. And that is only possible when the percentage in favour of a motion is exactly the same across every single local population – which is effectively impossible.

In situations where there is significant difference in political wills between populations, local control over government gives a massive benefit and many more people are happy with the law. In situations where there isn't significant difference between populations, local control of government still has more people contented with the law.

Scenario 3:

This phenomena doesn't exist only with situations where the largest population center gets what they want. It can also happen when the smaller population centers are able to get what they want against the wishes of the largest.

	Population 1	Population 2	Population 3
Population	1,000,000	2,000,000	3,000,000
In Favour	612,372(61%)	1,343,542(67%)	1,463,518(48%)
Against	387,628(39%)	656,458(33%)	1,563,482(52%)
Motion	Passed	Passed	Passed
% Happy	61%	67%	48%

In this case the motion passes with 57%. That means that 57% of the people are happy with the results. In this case, would locally controlled government still make more people happy with the law?

	Population 1	Population 2	Population 3
Population	1,000,000	2,000,000	3,000,000
In Favour	612,372(61%)	1,343,542(67%)	1,463,518(48%)
Against	387,628(39%)	656,458(33%)	1,563,482(52%)
Motion	Passed	Passed	Failed
% Happy	61%	67%	52%

Now 52% of the people in Population 3 have the law they want compared to only 48% under a centralized government.

Under all circumstances local sovereignty over government means more people have the laws that they want, and fewer people have laws that they don't want. A centralized government over multiple population centers means that fewer people are happy with the law and more people are unhappy with the law. A centralized government means less democratic power for everyone. Large geographies mean less democracy.

If anyone has the philosophy that we should do what's best for the majority – then we should have local control of government; as that is what brings what is best for the most people.

Governments Can Attempt Innovative Solutions with Localism

Sometimes an idea for a new social program can stir the imagination of people that might want to try that program. But sometimes that means great risk because of the sheer volume of people involved with a massive nation.

But a smaller, more local government might be willing to attempt that with less risk.

Let's imagine that people wanted to try to implement a form of Negative Income Tax. The idea might interest some people. Get rid of all social programs and just give money to lower income citizens based on their taxes.

Proponents of a Negative Income Tax believe that if we're going to be spending money on the poor anyway, we might as well save some money and make it more efficient via a negative income tax. They say that no one knows how to better spend the money and where it is most needed than the people who will receive the benefit, so we might as well get rid of the bureaucracy of welfare and just make it straight up cash.

They also say that by incorporating this system straight into the tax system, we can eliminate an entire section of government spending which is the bureaucracy of the welfare system.

These are all very interesting points that warrant consideration.

But critics are concerned that a negative income tax will reduce the incentive for productive work and people will become more complacent and choose to live off the negative income tax rather than being gainfully employed.

That's a significant risk. It would mean that the system will eventually fail as less money is going into the fund and more money is coming out of it.

So which is right? Would this type of a system save us billions of dollars in administration costs? Would it eliminate poverty traps while still providing a safety net for those that need it?

Many nations are afraid to even try such a system to see the results. That isn't unreasonable for if it fails it means a massive disruption to everyone.

But now imagine that instead of a massive, near continental nation such as Canada, or the USA, or China, or Russia with one central bureaucracy, we had small nations with local governments. In such a place we might have a nation that has very little unemployment and little risk of people choosing to abandon good paying jobs for less money, despite an easy, complacent lifestyle.

Since their policies would only affect themselves, they can choose to conduct such an experiment with significantly less risk of catastrophic failure.

In the event that they find the experiment failed and in fact it did increase people leaving the workforce to live off the work of others, then they can more readily cancel the failed experiment with fewer lives being disrupted in the meantime.

It is easier to change a policy back when only a few hundred people are affected than if a massive nation tried this same experiment and it now affected millions of people. That would be a political mess that no one will likely be changing back.

 This means that other nations can watch and learn from the failures and successes of each other. With more nations being free to make such attempts, we'd have more options available to us. We would have more case studies to see what policies work and which do not. If we only have a large, single government over everyone, we can only really implement one policy at a time. We can never really compare and contrast different ideas and see the results simultaneously.

 Large, centralized governments inhibit the ability for people to try new, innovative solutions to social problems. They force people to keep trying the same thing over and over and hoping for a different result. Small local governments are freer to experiment with less risk. They can also witness new and innovated policies in many different places and see which ones are working best and which they would like to implement for themselves.

Local Governments Can Implement Locally Effective Solutions

Sometimes what works in one place won't work in another. A government policy that might be very effective in one area can be disastrous elsewhere.

This could be due to differences in the economic environment, it could be differences in culture, wealth, or the actual weather.

But regardless of the cause, the idea that there are one size fits all solutions to social concerns just isn't true. Why then would we want to have government decisions made on a centralized level rather than having decisions that are specifically tailored to the needs and wants of a local population?

A local population knows better than anyone else what is important to them there. They know the concerns that are the most pressing. A landlocked area isn't concerned about dock procedures. And a prairie isn't concerned about avalanche prevention programs. The prairie folk want to focus on what is directly and immediately important to them.

One might say that the prairie folk aren't involved in those issues of avalanche control, and that is likely true. But perhaps a controversy is becoming a significant political battleground on that issue. Perhaps it is contentious enough that it will cost a federal election or win one, and that means the federal debate will be centered on it. Since the debate and focus of the election are on that issue, the needs of one people are being ignored due to this political necessity of addressing an issue that doesn't involve them.

That risk doesn't really exist when laws are controlled locally. While some people might not care at all about an issue even when local, it is very unlikely that a political debate will ever center around an issue that is disinteresting to the majority of people there.

A centralized, bureaucratic government is unable to make a policy that varies locally without spending a great sum of resources to investigate the best solution for each location.

Conversely, a localized government where the people have direct control knows what they need better than anyone else, and is able to implement their solutions readily and without great cost. The cost isn't there simply because they don't need to fund a study on most issues. They live with most issues every day of their lives.

If they find that their solution isn't adequate, they can adjust their solution more readily than if they have to go through a bureaucratic system to make that adjustment. They can fine tune their policies until it is optimal for their local needs.

Government policies aren't one size fits all for all people in all places. What works well in one area might not be best for another. By having control over government policy being as local as possible, all people are better able to have policies that best match the needs and circumstances that they are facing.

Nations Do Not Need a Coast to Be Sustainable

One fear among some with the idea of locally controlled governments is that they will no longer have a coast and therefore will be cut off from importing or exporting goods.

While it makes sense to be concerned about one's ability to import or export, whether one has a coast doesn't hold as much power over that ability as we might first assume.

There are many successful landlocked nations in the world. Switzerland, Austria, and Luxembourg are but three examples. They can all export and import across the world without any significant difficulties, and have been successfully doing so for hundreds of years.

They don't need a coast of their own to be able to export their goods. They need trade and transport agreements.

Being part of a larger nation doesn't protect you from export restrictions or tariffs.

The nation can still impose trade restrictions or tariffs on you when you are a part of the nation. In fact, this has happened very often in large nations such as Canada or the USA. The federal government has created a tax, tariff, or restriction which hindered the sale or export of goods from a state or province. There was little that could be done by those states or provinces except complain. If they had political might then their complaints might be heard from the government. If they don't then their complaints will be ignored. As demonstrated previously, under centralized governments many people often lack political power. Under local governments their political power is much stronger.

Having sovereignty gives more control over the power of import or export, not less.

A sub-sovereign entity must obey the central government. They don't have the ability to change the law except through the political process. However, given their weaker vote through centralized government, that power is often not truly effective. It is an illusion of freedom and power where it doesn't truly exist in a meaningful and effective way.

If that type of state or province doesn't have any political influence, due to geographic location or population size, then they are unable to change any policy which unfairly targets them or places restrictions or tariffs on their exports.

Now imagine if that small state or province were sovereign. Now instead of being told what the trade restrictions will be, they can negotiate what the trade restrictions can be. The reason they couldn't negotiate that before is that the central government can impose a tariff or restriction unilaterally. They have no legal obligation to negotiate it. Also, they have no reason to because that state or province had no political power so they don't really care if they are opposed there.

Whereas if that state or province were sovereign, they have no choice but to negotiate.

Will the small state or province have more or less power to influence the outcome of trade with a much larger neighbouring entity than they would as a sub-sovereign entity? They will have much more power. As above as a sub-sovereign entity, they have no power at all to protect their interests. They don't have the political power to change the policy. And when they are dictated a deal that is unfair they have no means to put any influence to change that.

But as a sovereign nation, they do have the ability to influence those agreements. Firstly just by the nature that this is a negotiation they have more influence. But also they actually have a power that they can use.

Unlike as a sub-sovereign entity, as a sovereign nation, they can treat the larger nation in the same manner that they themselves are treated. If the larger nation would impose tariffs on the smaller entity's exports, then that smaller entity can impose tariffs on all imports from that larger nation. That simply ability to reciprocate gives immense power that they were unable to apply before.

Since the larger nation will likely want to sell their goods and products to that smaller nation, they will now have to consider the costs of any tariffs on imports that will affect those sales. Having local control over government increases your ability to negotiate, it doesn't diminish it in the slightest.

International law demands access to ports for landlocked nations.

The UN Convention on the Law of the Sea includes a proviso that nations with a coast which border landlocked nations must provide access to that port to the landlocked nations without tariff. The risk of a nation being unable to sell its goods is not likely, and that is especially true if they are bordered by nations that respect the UN and international law.

Small sovereign nations don't need to have a coast to be viable. The only thing they need is a trade agreement. Given that their neighbours likely want to sell to them, and given the international law supporting granting access to the coast, it is very likely that they can all have trade agreements with each other.

Nations Do Not Need All Their Own Resources to Succeed

A misconception among some is that a nation needs to have every resource used in its economy under its jurisdiction to be viable.

This is generally not true as there are many examples where nations without all needed resources succeed. Like with most aspects, you don't need to have each resource yourself to be successful. You simply need trade agreements.

Singapore is a great example. Singapore has virtually no self-sustaining resources at all. It is a sovereign city state with nearly half the area of metropolitan Los Angeles. It doesn't have the farmland to feed its people. It doesn't have any mining or other excavation that will ever come close to meeting its demand.

And yet despite having no resources of note to export or even to use in its own industry, it is a massive success. It went from being a third world part of Malaysia to become an economic powerhouse in only a single generation.

Singapore simply imports every resource it needs for its industries. It doesn't need to have control over every resource that it uses for its own production.

Really that is also true of virtually all nations, even when they have all the resources they need within their own borders. Taking again an example from Alberta, there are massive deposits of iron in Alberta with more than 1.12 billion tonnes of iron ore. Yet Alberta imports the vast majority of its iron. This is very common among nations. They don't spread out their labour resources to mine each and every mineral within their borders. They specialize in a few and then trade with each other to be the most productive.

Even though nations grow wheat, they often import wheat. Even though nations often have iron in their nation, and they might even be extracting it, they will import iron. This simply maximizes cost efficiency.

It is this same method that allows small nations that don't have massive natural resources to operate without a problem, such as Lichtenstein.

Despite a location not having every resource used in its industry – and really that is true of most locations on Earth – they are still able to function perfectly well by trading with other nations.

Small Nations Can Manage Their Own Currency if Need Be

A small sovereign nation is able to remain sovereign and to manage their own monetary policy. A nation doesn't need to be large in either geography or population or even GDP to be able to manage its own currency.

Singapore has its own currency, despite having a land area of only the size of Los Angeles. Qatar has its own currency despite having a very small population of only 2 million people. Serbia is able to manage its own currency despite having a nominal GDP of only $38 billion – 1/359th that of the GDP of the Euro.

Most nations on Earth have used their own currency throughout history. This changed with the introduction of the Euro as it became a supranational currency. Then most European nations in the EU abandoned their own currency in favour of the EU.

A few nations did not. The United Kingdom did not adopt the Euro and kept the British Pound. This was despite being a member of the EU.

Switzerland also kept its Swiss Franc. Switzerland has a long history of independence which prevented them from even joining the EU when it was formed.

The Swiss Franc remained very strong despite being a currency of a very small nation of only 41,285 km^2 with a population of only just over 8 million. Being small in both population and area did not diminish the strength of the Swiss Franc.

Having a central monetary policy has both advantages and disadvantages. The main advantage is cost effectiveness. It is cheaper to maintain a single currency than many. This cost isn't prohibitive enough to mean that small nations should never choose to have their own currency, as indeed many small nations without large GDPs have been able to manage their own currency just fine.

A disadvantage is losing control over the monetary policy and how it relates locally. A large country can have very different needs in different areas and having one monetary policy for all can cause more harm than the savings are worth.

For example, in Canada, Toronto and Vancouver have ever increasing real estate costs that greatly exceed the rest of Canada. This is causing a potential real estate bubble. It also makes home ownership increasingly unattainable for those trying to own their own home – especially young people.

Another example would be inflation. One area in a country might be seeing prices increase dramatically and we might want to cool that inflation.

One possible solution to these problems could be to adopt a contractionary monetary policy and increase the bank rate.

That would make the cost of borrowing more expensive and would lower the costs of goods.

But if another area has the opposite issue – such as falling real estate prices leading to negative equity – that policy would be disastrous for them. Increasing the costs of mortgages while house prices are already falling will only cause them to fall faster.

Likewise for unemployment, a contractionary monetary policy would cause an unemployment problem to increase.

But if areas that had inflation, strong employment, and rising housing costs could manage their own monetary policy, and areas that had falling employment and real estate values could manage their own; there would be a net benefit for everyone.

What choices do small governments have in terms of a currency?

They can choose to have a supranational currency such as the Euro. This is a good cost effective solution and it makes it easier to trade among all the members using that currency. It isn't without its faults though. It reduces the sovereign power that people can exercise over the monetary policy of their currency. That is a trade-off that must be decided by the people.

They can use their own currency, even if it is smaller in circulation. Like the Swiss Franc, a smaller circulation currency can be just as effective as a larger one. This gives the most sovereign power over the monetary policy of the people. It is more expensive as you need to maintain a monetary policy, the currency production, anti-counterfeit methods, etc and bear the cost of all those yourself.

Sometimes a nation might be concerned about price differences and the price of currencies of nations with a great amount of trade. In that situation, they still have options that shouldn't prevent them from having their own locally controlled government.

They can use the currency of another nation. This is the cheapest option. Your nation bears none of the operational costs of production, monetary policy, or anti-counterfeit methods. All of those costs are done by the issuing nation. You also have the absolute least control over the monetary policy – which is to say none. Despite that lack of control, using another nation's currency is a very popular method throughout the world.

Another method is for a nation to have its own currency but to tie the value of that currency to the value of its trading partner. This is called a fixed exchange rate system. A benefit to it is that a nation can have the exact exchange rate it wants in comparison to its trading partner. If the other nations currency is stable, then this currency will also gain that stability. Since this method doesn't mean using the same currency exactly but using its value instead, that means the issuing nation still has its own currency. So if it chooses it can cease to fix the exchange rate to the other currency. That option isn't so readily available to nations that simply use other currencies directly. That also means this method still has the costs of producing and maintaining their own currency.

The choices of using other currencies either directly or via price fixing are not the best solutions, but they are available to nations that don't otherwise have the resources available to them where the cost of having their own money is less than the benefit.

Small nations have many options available to them in terms
of how they should manage a currency. They have options to
choose a small, local currency; to peg their currency against
another; or to choose to use a foreign currency. Having local
government control doesn't diminish the choices available in
terms of monetary policy.

Immigration Should Be Controlled Locally

The immigration policy which settles new immigrants into any area should only be controlled by the citizens that live in that area. It shouldn't be determined by people who don't live there and are therefore not affected by the policy at all.

We wouldn't want our neighbours to have the power to tell us who can and can't live in our own house. Imagine a street with 20 houses and the majority of people living there voted that you and only you should have 15 more people move into your house. You have to make room for them, and you must even feed them and keep the house clean.

No reasonable person would consider this a fair deal. But it is entirely democratic. The majority of people on the street voted in favour of it. The reason it is both democratic and unfair is that the vote is controlled by everyone, but can be used to only affect one. This is a prime example of a dictatorship of a majority.

The people in other houses shouldn't have a vote about who must live in your house at all. They shouldn't be able to force their will on another person, especially where this decision only affects that other person and not themselves.

 People who don't live in the area shouldn't have a say on the policies in that area.

 After the 2016 federal election in the USA, many people in California, and perhaps a majority of them, are unhappy with the US immigration policy. They would like to see a more open policy. People in California can't get the immigration policy they want, but they could with localism. Should those states be able to determine the immigration policy of California against the wishes of the majority of people there? No. Only people who live in California should have any power in determining who gets to immigrate into California. Conversely, the majority of people in the majority of states voted in favour of an administration with this new immigration policy. Should the people of California be able to dictate policy to the majority of states? I would say no. And the people living in California should have no power in determining the immigration policy outside of California.

 On the opposite side of this coin, there is an ongoing dispute between the Parliament of the European Union and Hungary in terms of immigration. Hungary wants to further restrict immigration into Hungary, but the EU does not. The people who don't live in Hungary shouldn't have the power to force Hungary to accept more immigration than the majority of people there would like. The immigration policy in Hungary should be exactly what the majority of people in Hungary want.

 The immigration policy of any area should be exactly as open or closed as the majority of people living there want it to be. People who don't live there shouldn't have the power to tell the people that do who can and can't be allowed to immigrate into it. People who don't live there aren't affected by the immigration policy of other places – they shouldn't have any say at all on it.

Just as we wouldn't want people who don't live in our house to have the power to force other people to live in our house against our wishes, the people who don't live in one community shouldn't have the power to determine who is allowed to move into that community.

Some people might think who lives in a community or not has less of an effect on that community than who lives in a house. But that isn't immediately evident. If a community has a higher than wanted level of unemployment, then adding more people will even further lower the value of employment. Employers will have more people to choose for each job and will be able to offer lower wages and still have them filled because the value of labour will have decreased. Whether or not people are able to get gainfully employed is not a trivial matter.

Just like any other aspect of law, self-determination and maximum citizen control over government policy are paramount. The people who don't live in one area are not affected by the laws in that area, but the people who live in that area are affected by those laws. Therefore the people who don't live in that area should have no control over those laws, and the people that do live there should have maximum control over those laws. Immigration policies are no different. They should be determined by the people living there and no one else.

Localism Is Not Infinitely Reducible

Each street in a city cannot have its own laws. Each household cannot have its own law. Each person cannot have a set of laws that applies only to themselves.

This wouldn't work.

It would be far too confusing and time-consuming to learn the laws for each street. Each person could just make laws that allow them to take advantage of their neighbours. And the cost of administering this would be enormous.

Laws require lawmakers, police familiar with them, judges, lawyers, and administration. It takes a significant amount of human resources to make all the requirements of a practical and effective legal system function. A single household wouldn't have the labour available for this. Neither would a single neighborhood.

To be able to be a locally sovereign population, the government of that population must have enough human resources to create, execute, and enforce laws. It must be able to provide police protection to the general public. It must be able to provide military protection as well.

A neighbourhood just can't afford all that cost.

But a larger body with a sufficient population can, and it doesn't need to be a massive body to be sovereign. It can be as small as a city and the immediate surrounding area.

The modern world actually has some excellent examples of this.

Singapore is a city state which is entirely sovereign. It depends only on itself for taxation, legislation, police protection and even its own military.

Analyzing Singapore and Canada provides some interesting comparison.

Singapore has a population which is about 1/7th that of Canada's.

Singapore has an area that could never compare with Canada's. It would need to go to the city level for that comparison. Singapore with its 720 sq km area is about the same size as Edmonton, Alberta.

Yet despite being so much smaller, Singapore is able to provide all the services and functions that Canada provides, and more.

Health care, education, police services, and even the military are handled by a sovereignty that is the same size as a Canadian city.

The shocking part is their military. Despite having fewer people than Canada, and being only the size of a city they have a much larger military than Canada does. Singapore has a standing army of 72,000 soldiers compared to 68,000 in Canada. They also have a reserve force of more than 1,000,000 soldiers, compared to Canada's 32,000.

At 5 million people, Singapore has a higher population than Edmonton or even Toronto. But even Edmonton could have a military with a budget approaching $2 billion if it used the NATO standard of 2% of its GDP. Considering the Canadian military budget is only $18 billion, we can see how a small population in a small area can provide as much or more to its citizens than a larger, centralized bureaucracy can.

While not infinitely reducible, the concept of local control over the government in order to maximize the democratic powers of citizens is reducible to a very small scale, even as small as a large city if we so choose.

The Minimum and Maximum Size for a Good Locally Controlled Government

In searching for the best size for a locally controlled government we need to weigh a few competing factors.

We want the people to have as much democratic power as possible. This requires a small geography.

But we need to be able to afford certain minimum public services. The people should be able to have their own hospitals, schools, police services, military, etc. To be able to pay for these services and to staff them, there is a minimum population that is optimal. Without a certain level of population, the people are unable to provide these for themselves. Without them, they are not truly sovereign.

A minimum population is preferred for a sovereign state. A population of only a million people can afford to provide all the services mentioned above, and also protect themselves reasonably with a military force. That is the minimum population size that is likely to be able to provide all services and equal quality equipment.

A population could choose to be sovereign even without this minimum level of people, even if it means they will not be able to afford the highest level of protection with the best equipment in health care or military; they might choose this due to an ethnic or cultural difference that they want to govern in their own manner. That is a legitimate desire and should be accepted; after all, the government is only legitimate when the people agree to be governed by it.

Looking at successful hyper-small sovereign nations, we can gather a minimum area as well for a population to be sovereign. Based on Singapore's small size, a minimum area of 25 kilometers by 25 kilometers can be a successful nation onto themselves.

That isn't to say that is necessarily the ideal, it is merely a likely minimum that will still be able to provide all the services a government should provide, as well as have an effective military that can defend themselves. Singapore matches all those conditions and is only the size of a large city. It is a reasonable metric to base as the smallest likely size for a successful sovereign state.

What are the upper limits in size we should accept? If large geographies reduce democratic power, we want to avoid them. What should we consider as the upper limit?

One aspect of a government is the ability of the people to assemble and to protest against the government. In a massive geography such as the US, Canada, or Russia, it is unreasonably impossible for people in the majority of the country to be able to go to the capital. It is simply too far away. This is another example of how a large geography dilutes democracy.

We want an upper limit that is preferably able to be reasonably attended by people with only access to bus or car travel. We want them to be able to drive to the capital, assemble and have a meaningful meeting, then drive home all within one single day.

That puts an upper limit of about 150 km away from the capital. In an eight-hour work day, that would be 90 minutes travel to the capital, five hours spent in it, then 90 minutes return.

So we want the furthest corner to be a maximum of 150 km away from the center. Depending on the shape of the borders, we'd have an area of likely around 20,000 to 70,000 km². That is the size of very successful nations such as Israel, Switzerland, the Netherlands, and Ireland.

If a nation has fewer than a million people then having a land area that gives a distance greater than 150 km is perfectly reasonable. An example for that would be Greenland. With only 56,000 people and a land mass of 2.1 million km², there is no way they could effectively reduce the geographic size by splitting the sovereignty as there simply aren't enough people to be effective by dividing the people into more sovereign states.

Localism Can Still Mean Cooperation with Others

Locally controlled governments have every ability and incentive to cooperate with their neighbours just as they would if they were under one overarching central government. They would benefit from increased productivity and lower costs with free trade agreements just as they would receive that benefit if they had the same government.

Localism doesn't mean isolationism.

Just as no man is an island onto himself, no nation can ever be an island separate from the world – despite how hard some might try.

Localist control of government simply means that the people that live in the immediate area have control over the laws, taxes, finances, and policies of the government of the immediate area. It means they don't have control over the government that isn't in their immediate area. They allow people that live elsewhere to also have as much control over their lives as possible.

Just because people don't live under the same government doesn't mean they can't cooperate completely. They can have free trade to increase the productivity of the division of labour. They can have financial alliances. They can even agree to cooperate on a monetary policy and use the same currency if they so choose. In fact, they can cooperate with others and accomplish anything that countries that aren't under the same government can accomplish.

You don't need to be under the same government to help other nations. International cooperation brought financial donations to Haiti after the earthquake in 2010.

You don't need to be under the same government to work cooperatively on mega-projects. International cooperation allowed Germany, the UK, and France to develop the Eurofighter rather than have one nation take all the financial risk on their own.

You don't need to be under the same government to build infrastructure. The UK and France jointly worked on the Chunnel to create a technological marvel.

Cooperation benefits all parties involved and helps each party advance their own position and progress. Just as many hands make for light work, so does cooperation among nations improve our successes.

Localism doesn't mean trade protectionism.

The benefits of a free and open trade system remain even if the government is controlled locally. It is in the best interests of all involved to have a fair and free trade system that doesn't give any side an unfair advantage and allows for a division of labour and production that benefits all trading partners. That will mean more productivity and cheaper costs for everyone involved.

Localism doesn't mean lack of free movement.

Just because nations aren't controlled by the same government doesn't mean they can't have a free or easy pass across borders.

Prior to the 9/11 terror attacks, the USA and Canada had a very open and easy border that didn't even require a passport to cross. The nations trusted each other's policies and people to such an extent that they didn't require much to cross the border. Usually, a local driver's license would suffice.

Likewise, if two small nations wanted to have easy border crossing or no restriction on border crossing at all, that remains available to them.

They might choose to change restrictions. Perhaps a major disease can be contained by implementing a temporary border guard. If there is a major outbreak in Area A that the people in Area B want to prevent from coming into their land, they can do that. That is something that would take much longer to implement in a central government.

Perhaps there could be an infestation in lumber or another flora or fauna that would devastate a local community. In that situation, they might want to establish a border crossing just to look for that infestation before allowing people to cross the border. Again, this is much more difficult under a centralized government.

Localism does mean others can't force you to partake in their programs unilaterally.

While all nations would remain part of the global community, localism does mean that the global community cannot unilaterally force you to obey them. Instead of using force on a policy, they must instead use persuasion. Instead of being commanded, you must be convinced. Localism fosters an environment of negotiation over one of political or even military dominance.

Localism doesn't mean isolationism; all people remain a part of the global community. It does mean that other people cannot force others into an action. They must use persuasion and negotiation. Localism doesn't mean trade protectionism. People would need to agree to a fair trade agreement that benefits everyone. But it does mean that others can't force you to buy from them at the cost of your own industry as well. Localism means that people can cooperate and find a mutually beneficial agreement that works for all based on negotiation, rather than one that is heavy handed and one sided which is forced on others due to political dominance.

Small Governments Can Still Protect Citizens with an Effective Military

Fear of having an ineffective military for protection due to being a smaller nation is not realistic. A large nation that reduces democratic power has no more a powerful nation than if it were split into a confederation of smaller nations each with their own armed forces.

If a nation has an army with 100,000 soldiers, and it were divided into a confederation of 10 independent, sovereign nations which were still united in cause and the mutual benefit and protection of each other, they would have the same strength in arms as a confederation or alliance as they would as a single, larger state.

In that scenario, if each smaller nation had roughly one-tenth the size of the original, it would be very reasonable to assume each could support one tenth of the originals armed forces of 100,000 – so 10,000 each.

Each nation now has an armed forces which add up to the same strength they had before.

Having separate but united armies doesn't mean ineffective leadership.

One concern would be that each army would not be able to function any longer as a holistic unit. This doesn't make much sense after any examination. Many nations use the same type of equipment so that they have common and interchangeable supplies and training. That should also be the case for any confederation of sovereign states.

Likewise many nations that have mutual defense treaties choose a general from among their nations to act as the over-arching commander of the allied defense force. For example NATO is composed of dozens of individual sovereign nations – the USA, Canada, the UK, Germany, and many others. Each of those is a sovereign nation with their own government, their own laws, and their own military. Yet they act in a unified force under the command of the Supreme Allied Commander.

Sovereign nations agree to this because it is in their best interests to have a unified command structure. This type of allied force means that smaller nations can form a much larger and more powerful armed forces through cooperation than they can each provide individually.

Smaller sovereign nations can collectively have an armed forces as large and well financed as they can if they were under a single government. They can have the same uniformity of equipment. They can have the same unity of command. There is nothing that many smaller sovereign nations can't do together that they could do if under a single government.

Many smaller nations are better protected than one large Country.

While it may seem counter-intuitive to some, a larger nation is more susceptible to take over from external threats.

Some think that a larger nation with its unified army under a single centralized command would be much stronger than many smaller nations, even if they were all working together and formed the same size together. But the opposite is actually true.

Smaller nations working together are stronger exactly because of their decentralized structure.

A larger nation has only a few targets that need to be taken over for the entire nation to fall. It has one government that needs to be destroyed. It has one command center.

Compare this to a confederation of many smaller nations. They have multiple targets that would need to be eliminated before the entire structure could come down. If one target, such as a government or command center of one nation is destroyed, they can rely on the resources of the others to keep functioning.

This concept has been demonstrated in history. During World War 2, Nazi Germany was intent on conquering the entire European continent. They made plans for each nation they intended to invade. When they focused on France, they knew if they made a quick assault on the capital the rest of the country would fall. They focused straight on Paris and conquered it in only six weeks. Just as they expected the entire country fell.

Conversely, they also made plans to invade Switzerland. Germany started planning the invasion of Switzerland, Operation Tennenbaum, on 25 June 1940, the day France surrendered. Hitler made a few feints of invasion into Switzerland, but never actually invaded, despite having a deep hatred of the Swiss system of government and nationhood. It isn't certain why the invasion never went ahead, but here are a few possibilities.

Switzerland was a country with only a fraction the size and population of France. But unlike France, Switzerland had a decentralized system of government. They had 26 different cantons which each had their own government. If you conquered one canton, that didn't mean the others would fall. They could keep functioning. This means that Germany wouldn't have a single target to quickly attack in Switzerland like they did in France. The Nazi's would have to fight each step of the way and take more time and casualties in the process.

Even the Swiss army was decentralized. The Swiss had a citizen militia system with nearly every household having a full powered battle rifle locked in a safe and ready for immediate action. Being able to muster a relatively large, ready for action army in only a few hours in each city meant that paratroopers would be almost completely ineffective.

These factors, combined with the difficult terrain in Switzerland, led German commanders to predict their estimated casualties would be around 200,000 dead – nearly 10 times the number of casualties in France.

L.K. Samuels summed the Swiss accomplishment up as "Switzerland, a nation no larger than Maryland, was able to deter invasion by one of the most powerful totalitarian war machines that history had ever witnessed."

Having many small, locally sovereign nations with their own armies will mean fewer violent conflicts, not more.

Some might worry that having many nations each with their own armies will lead to more wars, but the opposite is actually true. It will lead to fewer wars.

Having a single central government that controls the armed forces doesn't remove the chances of people within that area from fighting with each other. In fact, it might make it an inevitability.

If there is a place that has no political power, either due to a dictatorship, or due to a democracy where power is centralized away from them, then those people have no ability to self determination so long as they remain under the control of that central power. This is a good description of any geographically large country, even if it is a democracy.

If they are prevented from self determination from the others, and if their need for self determination is strong enough, then they might turn to violence as their last and only hope for self determination.

As an example of that, there are many more civil conflicts in the world today than there are international conflicts. Some of these civil wars are to depose of the government and replace it with themselves. But a significantly large number are based on one region wanting self determination as opposed to be controlled by others.

Having a central command didn't increase their stability. It forced instability.

However, if these groups had their own sovereignty from the beginning, then in many of these cases there would have been no need or even any desire for violence.

All wars are about getting power. So give the power to the people and they won't need to fight others. Nations that don't want others to rule over them and also have no desire to rule over others are no threat to each other. They will trade with each other and cooperate with each other.

The only people that would want to instigate violence against others that are not threatening them with violence in such a scenario are those that want to have power over other people; and free nations should stand united against any aggression from such people. If they stand united and defend their own freedom and that of others, they will have a massive force that will eliminate any chance for those that would want power over others to attempt to take it. That will again reduce the desire and frequency of violence within or between nations.

Having smaller but more armies doesn't decrease peace and safety – it increases it. A small nation with a strong defense and a decentralized system of government and armed forces was able to deter the Nazis from invasion. That is something even the UK and the USSR were unable to do. Having more nations that have their own army doesn't lead to more conflict, it eliminates one of the most common causes of armed conflicts – the need for self determination. Smaller, decentralized nations that cooperate together in mutual self-defense are not less safe from invasion than a larger nation with centralized governments. They are safer.

Optimal Freedom Resists Totalitarianism

Just as nations with a centralized government are more susceptible to being defeated in a military conflict against an aggressive invader, they are also more susceptible to takeovers from within by authoritarian tyrants.

To use an example from Nazi Germany again, Hitler and the Nazi party were able to take over all of Germany by really only taking over a single institution – the German government. Once that was accomplished they were able to gain complete control over every other institution in Germany and have complete control over the whole country, and everyone in it.

The same is also true of the Bolsheviks taking control over Russia. They only had a few targets of power that they had to defeat before they were able to control all of Russia.

But if we compare the Nazi take over in German to the attempted fascist takeover in Switzerland and we see a significant difference in consequences.

The attempt of an Anschluss in Switzerland via the Swiss National Front Party – which were Swiss Fascists - failed miserably. The National Front attempted to use the Swiss system of direct democracy but that worked against them.

They wanted to redesign the Swiss system more on racial, authoritarian, and nationalist lines rather than the Swiss democratic system. The Swiss people voted overwhelmingly against it. With such a display of public disapproval, one which cannot be easily denied or accused of bias like a poll sample, the Front National lost much of the credibility it was claiming for itself.

The Swiss dedication through both culture and law to individual freedoms also meant that the press was able to be very open in its criticism of Nazism.

Since each male citizen was by law a trained member of a local militia, and each was armed with a battle rifle locked in a safe at home, the Front National was unable to use any effective intimidation against the citizens by threatening them.

Totalitarians can take over large nations with only a few stress points. But if we moved sovereign power to a local community, there isn't a single stress point for totalitarians to take over. Their chance of failure increases with each new point of control. Each and every small government would limit the ability for a complete take over for everyone.

We Can Still Be the Same Country, Even If We Are Each Our Own Sovereign Nations

We don't have to abandon the concept or unity of being a single country to gain all the benefits of local sovereignty. We can be many locally sovereign nations that remain united under a single country.

How can we be many nations but a single country? Examine what the word nation means. One definition is a large body of people, associated with a particular territory, that is sufficiently conscious of its unity to seek or to possess a government peculiarly its own. That is a perfect description of any local population large enough to manage its own government. It also doesn't mean that such a body of people can't also be a member of a larger country – even where that larger country has no unilateral authority over them.

This concept is actually used in practice. In Canada, aboriginal communities are often called 'First Nations'. This is a good term as it reflects that they are a people onto themselves, and also that their people were in Canada first. They are a nation within a country. Unfortunately, this term is all lip service as it is applied in Canada as the First Nations lack the autonomous sovereignty that they, and all other people, deserve.

Also in Canada, Quebec is legally defined as a nation. It isn't a separate country, but it is its own nation. Unlike with the First Nations, Quebec does have more power over government and law. But they remain a sub-sovereign entity which means they do not have maximum democratic power within their own lands. That should change. They should have local sovereign power. Really, everyone on Earth should have maximum control over the laws that govern their lives.

A country with many smaller, locally sovereign nations would have a central government with very limited powers. The government that would preside over a country with many smaller, locally sovereign nations would not have any power to enforce laws on those local nations. Each of those local nations must maintain their sovereignty in order for the people to have maximum control over the laws that govern their lives.

What then would the role and powers of the centralized government be?

The central government can manage interprovincial, or interstate, or international (whatever term you want to apply) relations.

This must be based on mutually agreed terms. That is relations that were negotiated and accepted by all parties involved. For example, if some or all of those states agreed to free trade, but one state was violating that agreement, the centralized government would be a reasonable place to resolve that dispute – rather like disputing parties using arbitration. This would provide unity, clarity, and cost effectiveness, while also maintaining the sovereignty of each party.

Such a system is already in place in the form of the dispute system used by NAFTA. Even though Canada, the USA, and Mexico are all individually sovereign, there is an arbitration system established based on their mutual agreement. A centralized government can perform that role between member nations as well.

The centralized government can manage services that each member state needs and don't infringe on sovereignty at all.

There are many government services that can be shared among difference member nations even if they each control all the laws and policies of their own nations.

These services include:

- Postal services
- Copyright office
- Patent office
- Food inspection & regulation
- Drug inspection & regulations
- Any other service that doesn't infringe on the democratic will of any member nation.

These services don't take away from the power of the people to be able to determine the laws and policies that govern their lives. Sharing the costs and the benefits of these types of services can improve the efficiency for all and also help provide a service for some member states where that service would otherwise be prohibitively expensive due to their small size.

Despite having little or no restrictions on the democratic power of the people, member nations must still be able to opt out of these arrangements if they see it fit. Without that ability, even innocuous services like these can take away the ability of the people for self determination.

The central government can negotiate trade agreements with other countries collectively.

This is again cost effective and efficient. Each locally sovereign nation must have the ability to opt out of an agreement if they choose. Otherwise, they lose their sovereign power over trade. So be collective when it works for all, but allow each to opt out if they so choose. The ability for a sub-unit to opt out of an agreement already exists in Canada, where international treaties that affect issues under provincial jurisdiction are not enforceable by the Federal Government over the province. All treaties signed by the Federal Government must keep that in mind when being made.

If a centralized government is ever in the process of negotiation, and one of the member states wants to opt out, then the negotiation simply states that this agreement doesn't apply to that state, and the other states that want to proceed with this agreement are able to and are able to retain the efficiency of negotiating collectively.

The central government can manage diplomatic relations collectively.

Rather than each nation having an embassy of their own and negotiating diplomatic ties on their own, they can all collectively manage that function to save both time and money. Just as above, each nation must be able to opt out of any treaty and be free to manage their own diplomatic relations independently if they feel that their interests sufficiently disagree with the collective decision.

The central government can manage the monetary policy.

If nations chose to have a single currency, then that could be managed by the central government. The monetary policy would need to be determined based on a vote of all nations.

As discussed previously, having a central monetary policy has both advantages and disadvantages. Those advantages and disadvantages do affect the lives of the people of each nation, therefore, each nation must have the option to opt out of a shared currency and monetary policy in favour of managing their own if they so chose.

Centralized governments can manage the military alliance of all member nations.

Each nation would still control their own military but would be a member of a military alliance, just as each country in NATO manages their own military but is still a member of NATO. Like with NATO, each nation should be committed to each other's defense. They should provide troops to be stationed outside of their own borders and in the borders of the other nations to provide mutual benefit and protection. And an attack on one should be considered an attack on all and treated appropriately.

But unlike with a central government that has control over the military, the military of some nations cannot be forced into military action against the will of the people there. For example, with the invasion of Iraq in 2003, there were many people that objected. But those objections had no power as the United States Federal Government has complete control over the military. As such, everyone went to war, whether they wanted to or not. If each state had its own military that was united in mutual defense of the United States, each state could have decided for themselves to support the invasion or to stay out of it. Having the power to control the entire military in the hands of only a few people jeopardizes everyone.

Conversely, if our countries were instead formed into many small, locally sovereign nations and one of those nations had a war mongering leader, the rest of the nations can refuse to join that war effort. That means the war mongering leader is on their own. With less support, they are less likely to engage in such aggression. And if they decide to anyway, the other nations have the ability to kick them out of the country – meaning they won't be responsible for the consequences of that reckless behavior, and it will further show the lack of support for such a leader. Such nations would be on their own and would not enjoy the same strength of numbers in defense. This makes military aggression far less likely when compared to massive military power being held in the hands of a few people. Especially when those few people can be elected with only 20% of the people as discussed in the chapter 'Representative Democracies or Elected Oligarchies?'.

Each nation should have the right to opt out of a military action, or to opt out of the alliance as well. Military decisions affect the lives of the people in that country, and therefore the people should have maximum control over that decision-making process. That means local sovereignty must reign supreme. The people that choose to stand for each other will do so. The people that choose to stand alone will also do so.

A large country with a large army is more likely to be aggressive in military actions against others. Whereas an alliance of many small nations are less likely to be so aggressive. There is a strong possibility that some of those nations will object and not participate in the aggressive war. That would weaken the military strength of the aggression, making it less likely to go forward. But against an aggressor, the many small nations are very likely to honour their commitment to each other's mutual defense. If they do not, they know that they might be the next nation invaded. Such an alliance between nations to defeat aggressors is precisely the type of arrangement that unified nations all over the world to successfully rally against the aggression in World War 2. Smaller, allied nations are less likely to aggress, but equally likely to unify in defense.

The bottom line is that any mutually shared initiative must never take the maximum control over government away from the people by diluting each persons vote by large numbers of population and large geographic area. Services that don't restrict the sovereignty of small local governments can be shared among nations based on mutual agreement. Services such as patent registration and a postal service do not jeopardize the sovereignty of the member nations and so are very reasonable to share their costs and their benefits.

Even some systems that reduce but don't eliminate sovereignty can be adopted if the benefits outweigh the costs and they maintain the ability to leave the collective arrangement based on their own decision and not the decision of the other member states. Member nations must be working collectively only because they find it mutually beneficial, never because they are forced to against their will.

Foreign trade and diplomatic relations are examples of systems that can reduce but not eliminate sovereignty. Since they make agreements with other nations collectively, each state has less control over the agreements made. If those agreements are less than optimal for a particular member state but not so much that they would do better to negotiate on their own, then they can still accept the agreement. But they must not be in a position where they are forced to accept a deal that is against the will of the majority in their nation. They must be mitigated with an ability to opt out of the collective agreement and an ability to then form their own agreements outside of the collective one.

Shared monetary policies likewise can also weaken sovereignty. A decision can be made collectively that benefits one area over another. In all reality that has to be expected at all times as each market will not have the same performance as the others at all times. The choice of a shared monetary policy is one that the member nations must all make in a cost/benefit analysis. There are some benefits that might outweigh having a collective monetary policy even if that policy isn't optimal to a particular state. But also they must have the ability to opt out of that system with relative ease to adopt their own monetary policy in order to protect their sovereignty.

A common element of this type of arrangement is that countrywide systems are now made based on negotiation and mutual benefit, rather than a system forced by one larger population over a smaller one simply because the larger one has more political power due to their population size.

We can have both maximum control over government by adopting a system of small, locally sovereign nations and the benefits of being in a single country. We can have all the advantages of cooperation and unity while also gaining a maximum level of freedom. There is no conflict in having both local sovereignty and mutual cooperation on a larger supranational or even a global level. This isn't a decision of having one or the other, we can and should have both.

Large Countries Should Consider Transferring Sovereign Powers to Local Levels

Any country that has more than two million people and an area where the capital is more than 150 km away from the borders should consider giving more sovereign powers to the local levels so the people have more democratic powers.

The voting power of every citizen will increase.

If people have a central bureaucratic government with a large population and a large geographic area, then their vote is not as strong as it could be. Their personal influence on the law is less than it could be.

If a nation has ten million eligible voters over a large land mass, they could transfer some or all sovereign powers to a more local level. If they remain as they are, each citizen has $1/10,000,000^{th}$ of the power over law. If they moved sovereignty to two local levels instead, each citizen could then have $1/5,000,000^{th}$ of the power over the law. Each citizen just doubled their voting power instantly.

With the premise that every person should have as much democratic power as is reasonably possible, then this should be done as it does increase that democratic power.

Transferring sovereign powers to local levels does not mean the nation needs to break up.

As described in the last chapter, countries can be divided into smaller, locally sovereign nations while still remaining a unified and functional country.

Switzerland is a confederation which is built of 23 cantons, each with a large degree of sovereignty. But all in all most people don't think of Switzerland as being too different from any other nation.

Likewise, if the people of a large nation decide to have more sovereign control over their government and transition that power to their local level, they can still remain a part of the country they are in. The only thing that changes is that the laws will be determined locally instead of centrally.

Transferring sovereign powers to local levels decreases the risk of secessions.

Decentralizing government power and transferring that to create smaller, locally sovereign nations within a country doesn't mean a country has to break up. In fact, it decreases the chances of a country breaking up.

There is little need for a secession if the objective of self-determination is accomplished by decentralization of power. Ethnic concerns can be locally addressed. Economic concerns are locally addressed. All the benefits that people would want from secession is also achieved by sovereignty.

If you want to reduce the risks of secession in the future, move towards small, locally sovereign nations within your country now.

Everything that was enjoyed under a central bureaucracy can remain.

By giving each location much more and perhaps even sovereign control over the laws that affect themselves, they do not in any way diminish the connection and relationship that each location has to each other.

If the United States were to abolish the federal government in Washington D.C. and each state had sovereign power over themselves, they can still remain in and cooperate with a United States of America. It doesn't mean that they are abandoning unity. It doesn't mean they are any less allied or cooperative.

Their military can be divided to each of the 50 states and they would still have the exact same military might as they did with a federal government. They can still cooperate to defend the coasts and borders, meaning inland states can still send their troops out of their home state to help defend the coast for the mutual benefit of all.

The states can all agree to negotiate collectively under the banner of the USA with other nations in terms of trade, diplomacy, and defense; just like they do today.

If each state were sovereign, the only thing they would lose is a weaker vote. This would solve a massive element of political polarization as more people would get the government and the laws they want. They wouldn't have to force other people to accept a government they don't want. That's a benefit to everyone, not just a select few. Local government control only increases the connection people have to their laws and increases the number of people who are satisfied with the status of their government.

Support for Local Control of Government Is Growing

The desire to have control over your own destiny is natural and widespread. We can see that some movements looking to gain political independence from a larger nation are gaining more momentum. This isn't a new phenomena at all. In fact, it has been the general worldwide trend in the last 70 years. In 1946 there were 76 independent countries in the world. Today there are 193, nearly three times as many.

The most recent news breaking example is the referendum in England which choose to leave the European Union. A major factor in that decision was that the EU was capable of creating law in England without the ability of the people in England being able to accept, reject, or modify that law democratically.

In the United States, there has often been a desire in Texas to have control over the laws within Texas. The United States is an interesting political structure as it does have States which should theoretically have a very large degree of sovereignty. Really the only laws that the Federal Government of the US should be able to pass are those specifically dictated in the Constitution of the United States. But even there the States have often felt that the Federal Government is constantly overstepping and overreaching with its power.

The political desires in Texas aren't dissimilar from the US Constitution. Politically, if Texas were to become more sovereign then we would see little change in the day to day life of Texans. But they wouldn't have a centralized bureaucracy to fight with and to watch that it isn't overreaching its mandate.

Again in the USA, we see California growing a secessionist movement. Both Texas and California have large populations and a very large economy. They could both easily be powerhouse countries of their own. The movement for independence is often presented and thought of as the dislike of one spectrum of politics versus another. When the United States is federally very liberal that goes against the majority desire in Texas. When the US is federally very conservative, that goes against the majority desire in California. Some people might call this petty, but that's usually only people who agree with the federal government at the time. When the federal government is conservative, conservatives think it petty and liberals think it reasonable, and vice versa.

But it isn't pettiness to want to have control over the government. The constant unhappiness of either Texas or California can both be assuaged if each were sovereign and neither could impose law or policy against the wishes of the other. Texas and California, and all other states, could still cooperate for mutual benefit with each other on every issue of importance to them all.

Belgium has a strong possibility of being partitioned in the near future. Divided roughly right down the middle you have two distinct and competing populations. They have different political objectives and even speak different languages. The Flemish in the North and the Walloons in the South. Unlike what has been focused on in this book where one population can dominate another even in a democracy due to population differences, both of these regions have roughly the same populations and therefore roughly the same political power federally. That hasn't allowed them to escape the negative consequences of central, federal governments. Though neither side can dominate the other, they have been brought to a stalemate several times and have often become ineffectual.

A Partition of Belgium is a serious possibility. In fact, it is on the platform of the leading political party in Belgium at the time of the writing.

In Canada, Quebec has attempted to gain control over the laws of Quebec by having two separation referendums in the last sixty years. Each failed but by a very small margin.

If Canada were changed so that each province had sovereignty, but Canada remained as a true Confederation, think of how those separation attempts would be pointless. Think of the ability for Quebec to control its own culture and law based on that culture. Quebec shouldn't be forced to have the same laws or policies as the rest of Canada. They should be free to create their own laws democratically.

Also in Canada, there have been independence movements in Alberta. Alberta is very similar to Texas in a sense. It has a very large geographical area – only 5% smaller than Texas – and has a strong economy. Like Texas, there is a western/frontier heritage which respects independence. Alberta has only elected one separatist party member into the Alberta legislature. But the sentiment that Albertans should have the right to self-determination has been growing in Alberta. (Disclosure notice: The author is an Albertan advocate for transferring powers of sovereignty over Alberta away from the central government in Ottawa and into the hands of Albertans)

Catalonia has had a desire to separate from Spain and its separatist party won a majority of seats in the most recent election, while they fell just short of a majority of votes.

The Kurdish people want to have their own state rather than be under the control of both Iraq and Turkey. They have taken advantage of the civil war in Syria and Iraq to create a de facto sovereign state separate from Iraq.

These movements sometimes are based on ethnic differences, or based on cultural differences(this could be argued for every case, actually), or they are simply based not on cultural or ethnic differences but are based on the desire to have an increased control over the law. None of these differences has more legitimacy over the others. Even seeking sovereignty for what others might consider being a petty reason has legitimacy because it is the will of the people, and the will of the people should be the basis of law in each and every case around the world.

Each for their own reason, the concept of having increased local sovereignty is increasing worldwide. Sovereignty movements happen either through peaceful democratic change or through violent civil war. The latter only ever occurs where one group dominates another and refuses to give them self determination. If the democratic will of any people to be sovereign is accepted, there is never a reason for violence. When people do get local sovereign control over their governments both they get more power and the people in the rest of the country get more democratic power as well.

The Primary Role of Government Is to Protect Its Citizens

The first and highest function of the government is to protect its citizens. This is the reason people don't want to live without any type of law or government at all. It is a role which non-government agencies cannot do well.

There are very real threats in the world and a good government which protects its people can mitigate and reduce the risk of those threats. A bad government can increase them.

What role should a government take in protecting against threats? There are three basic protections a good government must provide citizens: protection from each other, from foreign threats, and from the government itself.

Protect citizens from each other.

There will be people willing to injure another to be able to benefit themselves. In many cases, these actions are illegal, such as assault, theft, murder, etc. One role of government is to make and enforce laws with the goal of minimizing these threats.

Another is to protect the individual rights and freedoms of people from being infringed by other people. No person should have the power or right to remove another's freedom of speech, or belief, or religion.

Even with individual rights and freedoms as well as maximum control over government, people can still live their lives without freedom if they are faced with non-governmental threats. Criminals, gangs, the mafia, and terrorism are a few examples. Non-government aggressors such as these prevent people from living freely wherever they interact with other people. In a nation where these forces are not mitigated with a proper police force, the people must act in accordance with the commands of the criminal elements in order to stay alive. Once these forces are strong enough they then start to erode at the personal freedoms of people. Criminals prevent freedom of association and assembly because they have taken over the public spaces. Freedom of speech is destroyed because terrorists threaten the very lives of those who say what the terrorists don't approve.

Once those fundamental freedoms are taken away then the loss of control over the government is inevitable. The people cannot even discuss issues that affect their government if they don't have freedom of speech. They can't effectively coordinate a political movement without freedom of association and freedom of assembly. They cannot have any real ability to control the laws that govern them. Without that ability, the criminal forces that have been able to reduce the freedom of the people will now be able to modify and shape government policy to their preference and to add to their power over the people. If the people don't have control over the government, what could stop the criminals?

A strong, honest, and dutiful police force is a requirement to have freedom.

It is needed not only to protect people during their everyday lives but also to maintain an environment where the people are able to exercise their rights as a prerequisite to democratic rule.

The duty of the police is to provide citizens the safety from violence while they are exercising their rights. If gangs or criminals or terrorists threaten people in order to prevent them from gathering or speaking or exercising any other right, and if the police do not protect the people from those threats, then the people have de facto lost their freedoms. It is the primary role of the police to protect the people from such threats.

Protect citizens from foreign threats.

A constant in human history has been war. While the world has become more peaceful now than in any other time in human history, the threat of war or invasion always exists.

Indeed, one major reason that there is less war now is that modern militaries are so capable of war that there is a major deterrent even for the world's largest armies to invade others.

Preventing war or invasion is a key role of government. Fighting against an invasion is as well.

An armed forces is essential for people to be free.

Just as there will always be people willing to hurt others for their own gain, there will also be groups of people and governments who are willing to as well. These malevolent forces will always exist in humanity, and if they are able they will subjugate others. For people to be free and remain free, they need to be sufficiently powerful to prevent being conquered from such forces existing outside their borders.

Free people can get that power by both having a sufficiently powerful armed forces and to have alliances with other nations with sufficient armies of their own. Each nation individually doesn't need to have the largest army on Earth. But the nations collectively need a collective armed forces that is powerful enough to at least deter an attack by making the benefit of an attack far less than the cost will be to the attacker. Even a small nation such as Switzerland was able to deter Nazi Germany from invasion. And even the small communist country of North Korea is powerful enough to cause any invader to seriously reconsider its options.

Form alliances with nations that share the same spirit of defense of freedom as you.

Strong alliances create a force that can be large enough to deter attacks even from the largest aggressors.

Good allies place the well-being and freedom of their citizens at the utmost importance. Be wary of allying with nations that are willing to disregard the well-being and freedom of their own citizens. They are willing to sacrifice human well-being and perhaps even human life for their own purposes. They are therefore likely to sacrifice your well-being, freedom, and perhaps your very life if that too would benefit them.

Good allies are willing to defend their freedom against aggressors. They have the will and ability to defend their land against foreign invasion. They spend an appropriate sum of funds on the military and have a reasonably sized army. An ally that doesn't prepare for its own defense should be reconsidered as an ally. They may cost your defense more than they benefit if your resources have to be spread thin to defend them more than others due to their lack of preparation.

Be very careful in allying yourself with aggressors. An ally should take every reasonable action to prevent instigating a conflict. Provocative nations make poor allies as they can draw you into a conflict or a war rather than help you prevent them.

The government must protect citizens from oppressive laws, and from the government itself.

Perhaps the most paradoxical role of the government is to protect the people from the government itself.

Violent crimes and war have caused millions of deaths in the world. But they pale when compared to the hundreds of millions of deaths that have been suffered directly at the hands of ruling governments on their own people.

In the 20th century, we had the world's two most violent wars in history with more casualties seen than any other war before. World War I saw about 17 million people dead during its five years. World War II saw about 75 million dead.

As massive as those numbers are, the deaths caused by governments on their own people are equally as heinous.

The Armenian Genocide in Turkey killed 1.5 million Armenian Christians.

The communist revolution in Russia killed 9 million people. While this isn't the government at the time killing these people, it is deaths caused by revolutionaries killing for the sake of creating their new communist government.

Once the revolutionaries did become the government, the newly established Soviet Socialist Republics killed another 20 million of their own people between 1924 and 1953 – excluding war casualties.

The National Socialists under Hitler killed 11 million people, again excluding war casualties.

Mao's communist revolution in China and the 'Great Leap Forward' killed 40 million people.

The Cambodian Khmer Rouge killed about 2 million people – nearly 25% of the population of Cambodia – to bring about its communist regime.

Governments are one of the largest threats to the lives and well-being of the people. Ironically, protecting people from government oppression is a principle function of good government. It does that by enshrining human rights and freedoms as the highest principle, giving as much power to the people as possible, and by separating the powers of government to prevent dictatorships.

Do not trust that your government cannot also become a dictatorship.

Historically speaking it is very unlikely that your country, however peaceful it is now, is immune from take over by a violent dictatorship. There are always those willing to take control for their own benefit.

Having a peaceful country now does not in any way guarantee that it will always be that way. And not having safeguards in place that will help hinder the advance of an autocratic government rather guarantees that it will eventually happen.

Germany was experiencing peace before it came under Nazi rule. Only a nation with a strong defense of democracy and democratic institutions can resist the tendency for dictators in government.

How can a government protect people from itself? When the government is corrupt and a risk to the people, when the government is run by those who would do harm to the people, as listed above, it obviously won't be interested in protecting the people. How then is this ever accomplished?

Only by restricting the ability of government to exert a force on people can the government protect the people from itself. That must be done in times when the government is run by honest people who care about their fellow citizens. Once a corrupt government is in power it is too late. At that point, such a government will do nothing to protect citizens, and there will be little that citizens will be able to do to stop it that will not cost the lives of many people.

Limiting Government Ability to Coerce the Public

To help prevent the government from ever having the ability to dominate the people, we need some safeguards in place. The principles of each safeguard should be defended against removal by anyone.

We need third party oversight into all government activities.

In order to keep the government accountable to the people, we need to have honest knowledge of the government's behavior.

The first step to this is a right to information. Any citizen must have access to any information or documentation that exists on the government with very few limitations. Those limitations should only be where that information would put people at risk, such as national defense or military intelligence, etc.

The next part of this is freedom of the press. The government must have no ability to determine what press is legitimate or permitted to access government information.

A police force is able to be corrupted just like any other institution. This means we also require a strong, independent oversight of the police coupled with procedures to protect the rights of citizens from police corruption.

People must have a right to a fair trial with due process.

The government must be prohibited from taking a person's life, liberty, and property without due process of the law. Due process can be expressed as the right to be treated fairly by the justice system. It prevents a government from abusing its citizens.

Article 10 of the UN Human Rights Act states it rather well. "Everyone is entitled in full equality to a fair and public hearing by an independent and impartial tribunal, in the determination of his rights and obligations and of any criminal charge against him."

A fair trial with due process has some fundamental elements:

1. The right to a hearing within a reasonable time frame.

The government must have limitations on the time period between being accused and their trial. The length of that period can vary based on the complexity of the case or the severity of the crime. But it must be a reasonable time frame.

Without this, a person could be held in prison indefinitely while 'awaiting trial'. That then becomes a means for a government to bypass due process. Even if a person wouldn't be in jail, a speedy trial is a necessity so they can move on and live a peaceful life without fear from a sword of Damocles hanging over their heads.

2. People must have a presumption of innocence.

A presumption of innocence means that people don't have to prove that they aren't guilty of crimes they are accused of. Rather the government must prove they are guilty. And the standard of that proof must be very high to prevent innocent people from being persecuted by the government.

3. The evidence of guilt must be beyond any reasonable doubt.

That standard must be so high that any reasonable person who heard all the facts and arguments would agree that the person is guilty of the crime. This helps enforce the presumption of innocence and prevent the government from being able to prosecute a person on flimsy evidence.

4. The people need real and effective access to the court system, including a right to an attorney.

Everyone must have the right to defend themselves in person or by representation. Having a legal representative act on behalf of the defendant is a cornerstone of free nations. It is a means to prevent the government from summarily throwing people in jail or even killing them.

The people need a right to an attorney so that they are not maneuvered into an admission of guilt for a crime they didn't commit. They need an attorney to attack any false or illegally procured evidence.

If a person is unable to afford an attorney, then they need to have the state provide one to act on their behalf.

5. The government must prove not only that a crime was committed, but that it was also committed with a guilty mind.

In order to be guilty of a crime, a person must also have a guilty mind which led to the crime. This is called a *mens rea* in legal parlance.

This is an important concept in freedom because it acknowledges the difference between an innocent accident and intentional harm.

For example, if a driver hits someone with no fault of their own – meaning they weren't attempting to hit someone, and they took every reasonable precaution from hitting someone, then that person is not guilty of a crime.

If that person did intend to hit someone, then that person is guilty of a crime.

A middle position also exists here. If a person didn't intend to hit someone, but was recklessly negligent and didn't take reasonable precautions to prevent that, that person could be guilty of a crime as well. The guilty mind in that case rests in the reckless negligence. If in the above example the person hit was killed, then this distinction can make the difference between a murder conviction which needs guilty intent, and a manslaughter conviction which needs reckless negligence.

A person can still be liable for civil damages even without a proof of *mens rea*.

6. There must be a hearing before an independent and impartial court

While the court must be subject to the law as determined by the government, it needs to also be independent from it to prevent a government from being able to arbitrarily prosecute people.

The government cannot have an ability to influence a court in finding a person guilty. Otherwise, the government will have the power to put its political opponents in jail, not directly for political opposition, but with an illusion of justice.

Likewise, a government must not have an ability to influence a court in finding a person not guilty. Otherwise, it can use its power to keep its political allies from facing justice.

Additionally, the judge presiding over each case must be impartial to either the plaintiff or the defendant. Without this, there will be no sense that there has been a fair trail.

7. The applicant must have a real opportunity to present his or her case or challenge the case against them.

This will require access to an opponent's submissions, procedural equality and generally requires access to the evidence relied on by the other party.

This also includes the right to cross-examine any witnesses and witness testimonial.

8. A right to be tried by one's peers.

Juries act as an important curb against state power. They are a democratic power in themselves. The government cannot put a person in jail with a trial by jury if the jury considers them not guilty.

The government cannot apply a law against an accused if the jury finds the person not guilty because the jury thinks the law is unfair. In a very real sense, juries are the final bulwark against tyrannical laws.

A major role of the government is to protect its citizens from tyranny. Which is to say to protect citizens from the government itself. This is done by enshrining rights to the citizens, having a legal procedure which prevents government authoritarianism and giving citizens the power and method to exercise their rights.

Conclusion

Optimal freedom means that each person is as free from force or coercion on how to live their own lives as is reasonably possible.

People must have their own individual rights and freedoms which limit restrictions on what a person wants to be, wants to think, believe, or say. Ultimately, the only restrictions to one's actions should be where they would cause real injury or significant risk to another person or take away another person's rights and freedoms.

People should have maximum control over the government. That requires having ultimate power over government rest in the hands of the majority of people. While we can have an elected government, the decisions of that government must never be allowed to be against the wishes of the majority.

Governments must be as local as possible in order for each vote to have maximum impact on the laws that govern the people. The larger the population, and the larger the geography, the less power each vote has. For people to have maximum control over the government, they need a government that is as locally controlled as is reasonably possible.

The people need to have security to be able to effectively maintain their democratic power. A police force that enforces the law of the people and maintains law and order and a military that dissuades foreign invasion are both essential to democracy.

There must be protections for the people from government tyranny itself. Due process and the right to a fair trial are essential to keep both society and individuals free.

Each of these is a fundamental element of a free and democratic nation. If any of them are missing, our freedom and democratic powers are weak; and we remain vulnerable to oppression from a dictatorship of the majority, a takeover from a tyrant, mob rule, or being violently conquered by a hostile nation. Only with individual freedoms, maximum control over government, and security are we optimally free.

Jeff Rout is an Albertan author who focuses on philosophy, finance, and politics. He is the founder of the political party Alberta Freedom which focuses on maximizing the direct democratic control that Albertans should have over the government.

www.ingramcontent.com/pod-product-compliance
Lightning Source LLC
Chambersburg PA
CBHW021829020426
42334CB00014B/552